JOHN WAYNE

IN THE MOVIES

JOHN WAYNE

IN THE MOVIES

A RETROSPECTIVE BY TIMOTHY KNIGHT

METRO BOOKS
NEW YORK

DESIGNER: Les Krantz with Julie Nor
CONTRIBUTING WRITERS:
Ken DuBois, Michael Fox, Pam Grady, Dennis Kwiatkowski, Sheila Lane,
Ross M. Levine, Debra Ott, James Plath, Tim Sika and Christopher Varaste
COPY EDITORS: Katherine Hinkebein, Janet W. Morris
PHOTO EDITORS: Debbi Andrews, Thomas Jensen
EDITORIAL ASSISTANT: Katie Gates
DVD DOCUMENTARY:
Les Krantz (Executive Producer), Jack Piantino (Video Editor)
Kristie Back (Musical Selections)

METRO BOOKS
122 Fifth Avenue
New York, NY 10011

ISBN-13: 978-1-4351-1856-0

Library of Congress data available on request

Printed and bound in China by PWGS

1 3 5 7 9 10 8 6 4 2

DEDICATION

For my parents,
William and Mary Ann Knight

ACKNOWLEDGMENTS

I received invaluable advice and assistance from many people while working on this book/documentary package. First and foremost, I am especially grateful to Les Krantz, my mentor and frequent collaborator, whose persistence and vision made *John Wayne in the Movies* possible. Thanks also to copy editors Katherine Hinkebein and Janet W. Morris, designer Julie Nor and photo editors Debbi Andrews and Thomas Jensen for their exemplary work. Kudos to Jack Piantino and Kristie Back for skillfully assembling and editing the accompanying documentary, and to Jeff Joseph of Sabucat Productions for providing the footage. I am also grateful to Katie Gates for providing editorial assistance. Finally, my sincere thanks to everyone at Barnes & Noble for their good judgment and support; I am especially indebted to Cynthia Barrett, Mark Levine and Peter Norton.

It was my great good fortune to work with a crackerjack team of writers on *John Wayne in the Movies*. I cannot thank them enough for their sterling contributions and prodigious work ethic. I tip my hat in gratitude to Ken Dubois, Michael Fox, Pam Grady, Dennis Kwiatkowski, Sheila Lane, Ross M. Levine, Debra Ott, James Plath, Tim Sika and Christopher Varaste.

Scores of online and print sources were checked and cross-checked in the researching and writing of *John Wayne in the Movies*. Aside from the websites imdb.com, tcm.com and rottentomatoes.com, the *New York Times* online archive and the Academy Awards database, the following books provided the bulk of the information on Wayne's life and career: *The Complete Films of John Wayne* by Steve Zmijewsky, Boris Zmijewsky and Mark Ricci (The Citadel Press, 1983); *Duke: The Life and Image of John Wayne* by Ronald L. Davis (University of Oklahoma Press, 1998); *The Invention of the Western Film* by Scott Simmon (Cambridge University Press, 2003); *John Ford: Hollywood's Old Master* by Ronald L. Davis (University of Oklahoma Press,1995); *John Wayne: American* by Randy Roberts and James S. Olson (Bison Books, 1997); *John Wayne: The Man Behind the Myth*, Michael Munn (NAL Hardcover, 2004); *John Wayne: My Life with the Duke* by Pilar Wayne with Alex Thorleifson (McGraw-Hill, 1987); *John Wayne's America: The Politics of Celebrity* by Garry Wills (Simon & Schuster, 1997); *Shooting Star: A Biography of John Wayne* by Maurice Zolotow (Simon and Schuster, 1974); and *Who the Devil Made It* by Peter Bogdanovich (Knopf, 1997).

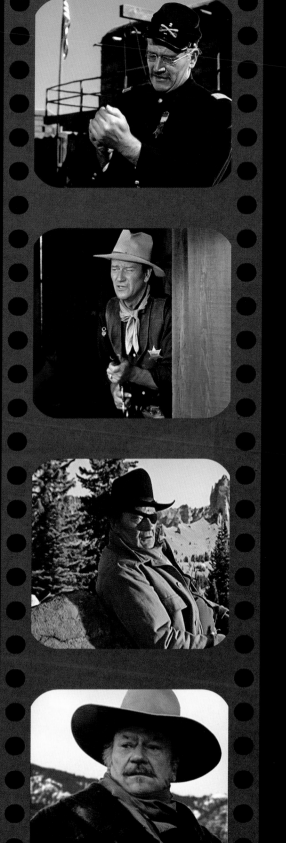

TABLE OF CONTENTS

Acknowledgments	vi
Introduction	8

PART 1 - 1939-1949   11

Stagecoach	18
Dark Command	24
Seven Sinners	26
The Long Voyage Home	28
Reap the Wild Wind	30
The Spoilers	32
Flying Tigers	34
Pittsburgh	36
The Fighting Seabees	38
Back to Bataan	40
They Were Expendable	42
Angel and the Badman	44
Fort Apache	46
Red River	50
3 Godfathers	56
Wake of the Red Witch	58
She Wore a Yellow Ribbon	60
Sands of Iwo Jima	64

PART 2 - 1950-1959   71

Rio Grande	76
Operation Pacific	80
The Quiet Man	82
Island in the Sky	86
Hondo	88
The High and the Mighty	90
The Sea Chase	92
Blood Alley	94

The Searchers	96
Legend of the Lost	102
Rio Bravo	104
The Horse Soldiers	110

PART 3 - 1960-1969   113

The Alamo	118
North to Alaska	120
The Man Who Shot Liberty Valance	122
How the West Was Won	128
Donovan's Reef	130
McLintock!	132
Circus World	134
In Harm's Way	136
The Sons of Katie Elder	138
The Green Berets	140
True Grit	142
The Undefeated	148

PART 4 - 1970-1976   151

Rio Lobo	156
Big Jake	158
The Cowboys	160
The Train Robbers	162
McQ	164
Brannigan	166
Rooster Cogburn	168
The Shootist	170

Filmography	176

INTRODUCTION

John Wayne reportedly loathed horses. Nor did he ever serve one day in the military. Yet the Iowa pharmacist's son born Marion Michael Morrison came to embody two of the most enduring archetypes in American popular culture: the cowboy and the gung-ho war hero. Even today, 30 years after his death from cancer, Wayne still casts a towering shadow, not just in film, but in American life and politics. He is often invoked as a symbol of patriotic might and conservative values — a powerful reminder of an earlier, supposedly *better* time in American history, when dedication to God and country prevailed.

Such a narrow perception of Wayne, however, diminishes both the man and his extraordinary film career, which spanned 50 years and more than 150 feature films. Simply put, he was far more than the sum of his arch-conservative, flag-waving parts. The 1920s-era University of Southern California football player who began his career as a prop boy gradually developed into a commanding actor of far greater subtlety than many critics initially recognized. Under the

WAYNE'S GREATEST PERFORMANCES

TOM DUNSON
Red River (1948)

In the first of five films he made with director Howard Hawks, Wayne gives one of his most complex performances as Tom Dunson, the aging cattle driver festering with resentment toward his foster son, played by Montgomery Clift. Wayne's powerhouse portrayal of the angry and conflicted Dunson in this superior western earned the Duke rave reviews; *Variety*'s critic pronounced his performance "magnificent."

SERGEANT JOHN M. STRYKER
Sands of Iwo Jima (1949)

Wayne received his first Academy Award nomination as the hard-driving yet caring United States Marine Sergeant John M. Stryker in Allan Dwan's box office hit. Expertly revealing the humanity beneath Stryker's bravado, Wayne may have lost the Best Actor Academy Award to Broderick Crawford in *All the King's Men* (1949), but the Duke won over even some of his toughest critics with his performance in *Sands of Iwo Jima* (1949).

SEAN THORTON
The Quiet Man (1952)

As the title character in John Ford's beloved adaptation of the Maurice Walsh short story, Wayne delivers an understated and heartfelt performance of tremendous charm. Playing an American boxer returning to his Irish birthplace, the Duke sets off fireworks with his greatest leading lady, Maureen O'Hara; the two share one of the all-time great screen kisses in *The Quiet Man*, which Ford shot on location in the Emerald Isle.

exacting, sometimes borderline abusive direction of his mentor John Ford, Wayne gave some of the screen's most indelible performances in such landmark films as *Stagecoach* (1939), *The Quiet Man* (1952) and *The Searchers* (1956).

Although Ford kick-started Wayne's film career by using him as an extra in a handful of silent films, it was director Raoul Walsh who gave the 23 year-old newcomer his first lead role in the big-budget western *The Big Trail* (1930). Billed for the first time as John Wayne — a name change suggested by Walsh — the inexperienced actor took on the demanding role of a western scout in a genuinely epic production. Shot in both 35mm and in Fox Grandeur, an early version of the widescreen 70mm process, on location in seven states, *The Big Trail* was supposed to launch Wayne into the cinematic stratosphere. But the film's critical and commercial failure instead consigned him to the Hollywood equivalent of purgatory: Poverty Row, the B-movie studios where Wayne languished for nine years, filming lowbudget western serials, until Ford came to his professional rescue and cast him in *Stagecoach*.

> "In an age of few heroes, he was the genuine article."
>
> — President Jimmy Carter after Wayne died

Ethan Edwards
The Searchers (1956)

Four years after *The Quiet Man* (1952), Wayne reteamed with Ford to tackle what is arguably the most difficult role of his career: Ethan Edwards, whose obsessive quest to find his kidnapped niece consumes him emotionally and psychologically, filling him with racist hatred for her Comanche kidnappers. In a lesser actor's hands, Edwards might have come across as a one-note character, but Wayne sug-

Rooster Cogburn
True Grit (1969)

Wayne finally won his long-overdue Academy Award for his superb performance as the one-eyed, whiskey-swilling marshal Rooster Cogburn in Henry Hathaway's enthralling *True Grit* (1969). Shedding all traces of movie star vanity, Wayne clearly revels in playing Cogburn, a paunchy, frequently soused old cuss who's still got the "true grit" to help a young woman track down her father's killer.

J. B. Books
The Shootist (1976)

Although in frail health, Wayne nevertheless summoned the fortitude to end his five-decade career on a high note with *The Shootist* (1976). He's remarkably moving as the title character, a legendary gunman dying of terminal cancer in Carson City, Nevada, circa 1901. Don Siegel's elegiac character study pays affecting tribute to the Duke, who lost his own battle with cancer in 1979.

John Wayne in the Movies: A Retrospective examines Wayne's career from *Stagecoach* to his last film, *The Shootist* (1976). Encompassing 50 films from this 37-year-period, it highlights the Duke's most revered films, from his "Cavalry Trilogy" with Ford to the Duke's classic collaborations with Howard Hawks and Henry Hathaway. Admittedly, some of the films are dated, racist, jingoistic and chauvinistic by contemporary standards. And a few would be downright forgettable — if not for the presence of Wayne, an American icon whose larger-than-life image is burned permanently into memory. Enjoy!

Former child star Shirley Temple and her future husband John Agar with Wayne in *Fort Apache* (1948).

"I've been in more bad pictures than just about anybody in the business. But it doesn't matter. As long as you project yourself, and you're not mean or petty, the public will forgive you."

— Wayne

Top: Wayne and Maureen O'Hara in their first film together: *Rio Grande* (1950). Bottom: Two Hollywood legends, Wayne and James Stewart, in John Ford's *The Man Who Shot Liberty Valance* (1962).

PART 1

1939-1949

OHN WAYNE: 1939-1949

here is a moment in *Stagecoach* (1939) when the camera sweeps toward a lone cowboy standing in the desert scrub. The man, of course, is John Wayne playing the Ringo Kid. Eleven years after first meeting *Stagecoach*'s legendary director, John Ford, and years after starring in *The Big Trail* (1930), the film that almost killed his career, Wayne finally ready for his close-up and became a major star.

The relationship between Ford and Wayne was a volatile one. Ford was often abusive Wayne, yet the two retained a friendship and a successful professional partnership. In the 0s they made several films together, including two of Ford's "Cavalry Trilogy" pictures, *Apache* (1948) and *She Wore a Yellow Ribbon* (1949). The two also collaborated on such s as *The Long Voyage Home* (1940) and *They Were Expendable* (1945).

WAYNE'S LEADING LADIES, 1939-1949

ENE DIETRICH
nners (1940), *The Spoilers*
nd *Pittsburgh* (1942)

"box office poison" by motion
exhibitors in 1938, the legend-
en siren made a triumphant
k in the western *Destry Rides*
939). She continued to mix grit
our in such 1940s-era films as
r (1941), co-starring Edward G.
and George Raft, and her three
Wayne, who fell hard for Diet-
stars carried on a steamy affair

JOANNE DRU
Red River (1948) and *She Wore a
Yellow Ribbon* (1949)

Remembered today chiefly for *Red River*
(1948) and *She Wore a Yellow Ribbon*
(1949), Dru also starred in the Academy
Award–winning *All the King's Men* (1949).
Despite generally fine notices for her performances in these films and John Ford's
Wagonmaster (1950), Dru never became
a full-fledged star. As her career faded,
Dru turned to television, where her
younger brother, Peter Marshall, found

PAULETTE GODDARD
Read the Wild Wind (1942)

Charlie Chaplin's onetime muse, wife
and co-star in *Modern Times* (1936) and
The Great Dictator (1940), Goddard was a
finalist for the iconic role that eventually
went to Vivien Leigh: Scarlett O'Hara in
Gone with the Wind (1939). The vivacious
and darkly pretty actress worked steadily
in the 1940s, earning a Best Supporting
Actress nomination for *So Proudly We Hail*
(1943), and raves for her performance

Throughout World War II, Wayne worked with various directors and starred in numerous films depicting brave and true American servicemen. Movies such as *Flying Tigers* (1942), *The Fighting Seabees* (1944), *Back to Bataan* (1945) and *Sands of Iwo Jima* (1949) led American audiences to view Wayne as synonymous with the roles he played, and catapulted him into the upper reaches of stardom.

After the war, Hollywood began struggling with the influence of Communism and the actions of the House Un-American Activities Committee. Wayne was initially apolitical, but by the late 1940s he became a leader in the Motion Picture Alliance for the Preservation of American Ideals — a conservative organization determined to fight Communism and preserve the American way of life. Wayne's distaste for Communism and even the "big government" of liberals was both philosophical — he placed a high value on individual freedom — and practical — he deplored the exorbitant taxes he paid.

SUSAN HAYWARD
The Fighting Seabees (1944)

The Brooklyn-born beauty with the husky voice and gutsy personality played essentially decorative roles until 1947, when her searing performance as an alcoholic singer in *Smash Up: The Story of a Woman* earned Hayward her first Academy Award nomination. Eleven years later, she won the Best Actress Academy Award for playing Death Row inmate Barbara Gra-

GAIL RUSSELL
Angel and the Badman (1947) and *Wake of the Red Witch* (1948)

A hauntingly beautiful actress, Russell never realized her full potential onscreen. Reportedly insecure and pathologically shy, she turned to alcohol to quell her nerves and descended into alcoholism. Although Wayne later cast her in a western he produced, *Seven Men from Now* (1955), Russell tragically continued her downward spiral and died at the age of

CLAIRE TREVOR
Stagecoach (1939), *Allegheny Uprising* (1939) and *Dark Command* (1948)

Trevor's career spanned from the 1920s to the late 1980s and encompassed stage, film and television. A fine actress who often played the "bad girl," Trevor received the Best Supporting Actress Academy Award playing a boozy aging moll in *Key Largo* (1948) opposite Humphrey Bogart; she had previously worked with Bogie on *Dead End* (1937) and *The*

Offscreen, Wayne led a complicated personal life. At the beginning of the 1940s, he was married to Josephine Saenz, who bore him four children. However, by the end of the decade, he had conducted an extended affair with Marlene Dietrich, met Esperanza "Chata" Baur, divorced Saenz, and married Baur.

To his critics, the larger issue in Wayne's personal life was his response to the American involvement in World War II. In 1941, just as Wayne's career was switching into a higher gear, the Japanese bombed Pearl Harbor. Many of the leading male actors of the day enlisted in the armed services, including Henry Fonda, Clark Gable and James Stewart. Initially, Wayne was exempt from the draft as the father of more than two children — a circumstance shared by others who enlisted anyway. Later, when the Selective Service reclassified Wayne as eligible, Herbert Yates, the head of Republic Pictures, fought to keep Wayne stateside by lobbying the government and threatening Wayne with breach of contract if he enlisted. Wayne did tour with the USO to visit the troops, but the fact remains that John Wayne, the man who came to epitomize the ideal American serviceman on-screen, never served a day in the military. This paradox haunted Wayne his entire life.

"Nobody could handle actors and crew like Jack. He was probably the finest artist I've ever known."

— Wayne on John Ford

Wayne in his breakthrough role: the Ringo Kid in *Stagecoach* (1939).

Top: The pride of the Marines: Wayne in *Sands of Iwo Jima* (1949). Bottom: The Duke in *3 Godfathers* (1948).

STAGECOACH (1939)

WARNER BROS. PICTURES

DIRECTOR: JOHN FORD

SCREENPLAY: DUDLEY NICHOLS

PRINCIPAL CAST: JOHN WAYNE (RINGO KID), CLAIRE TREVOR (DALLAS), THOMAS MITCHELL (DOC BOONE), JOHN CARRADINE (HATFIELD), ANDY DEVINE (BUCK), LOUISE PLATT (LUCY MALLORY), GEORGE BANCROFT (MARSHALL CURLY WILCOX), DONALD MEEK (SAMUEL PEACOCK) AND BERTON CHURCHILL (HENRY GATEWOOD)

John Wayne met the man who would make him a screen legend while working as a poultry wrangler on John Ford's *Mother Machree* (1928). As a prop man chasing geese around the set, Wayne didn't much impress Ford at first, but they bonded over time. Eleven years later, with countless drinks and card games shared between them, Ford decided it was time to make his friend a star.

Wayne's career had become stalled in a seemingly endless string of B-movie bit parts, and his confidence was hitting bottom; when Ford described his plans to make *Stagecoach*, Wayne suggested Lloyd Nolan for the part of the Ringo Kid. Ford offered the part to Wayne, then helped him get a new agent and went to battle with studio executives who were adamant that Wayne, a 30-year-old with an unimpressive on-screen résumé, was not at all what they had in mind. Ford secured marquee actors for other *Stagecoach* roles, and the studio let him have his way.

Top: Doc Boone (Thomas Mitchell) is happy to become acquainted with whiskey salesman Samuel Peacock (Donald Meek) and his case full of samples. Bottom: The gambler Hatfield (John Carradine) eyes the other stagecoach passengers and figures his odds.

Filmed on location in Monument Valley, Arizona, *Stagecoach* is an intimate, character-driven story carried out against some of the most expansive and beautiful scenery ever captured on film. Across this desolate stretch of desert, a stagecoach travels from one small town to another, loaded with passengers whose only connection, at first, is their need to get where the coach is headed. The story gets underway quickly after the nine characters are introduced: The no-nonsense Marshall Curly Wilcox (George Bancroft), who rides shotgun on the buckboard next to the talkative driver Buck (Andy Devine); the rummy Doc Boone (Thomas Mitchell) and a prostitute named Dallas (Claire Trevor), both of whom are on the road because they've been run out of town; a meek-mannered whiskey salesman named Peacock (Donald Meek) with an ever-shrinking collection of samples; the snobbish Mrs. Mallory (Louise Platt), heavy with child; the dubious gambler Hatfield (John Carradine); and the crooked banker Gatewood (Berton Churchill), clinging to his satchel of stolen cash. Along the way they pick up the Ringo Kid (Wayne), famous in the region for his recent jailbreak and headed for a showdown with the men who killed his father and brother. In the tight quarters of the stagecoach, and at the occasional oasis along the way, allegiances are made — for comfort, protection or whiskey — and the true nature of each character is revealed. The Ringo Kid, it turns out, is not the vicious villain he's rumored to be, but a sensitive sort

Top: Buck (Andy Devine) drives the six-horse stagecoach with Marshall Curly Wilcox (George Bancroft) at his side. Bottom: Aboard the coach, passengers Dallas (Claire Trevor) and Lucy Mallory (Louise Platt) endure a lecture from crooked banker Henry Gatewood (Berton Churchill).

who falls for Dallas right from the start. He's a sure-shot, too, which turns out to be just what the group needs when they're attacked by Apache warriors in the journey's final leg.

Wayne's dynamic entrance as the Ringo Kid.

The simplicity of *Stagecoach,* and the close proximity of the characters, gives it the distinct feeling of a stage play, with dialogue moving the story more than action. It works beautifully, and Ford's impeccable casting is largely the reason why. Claire Trevor, who was the biggest name in the cast and received top billing, is charming and sympathetic as Dallas, especially after we see her shamed by the local prigs; Thomas Mitchell as the jolly drunk Doc Boone is a scene-stealer, conniving and joking — and drinking — right up until the moment duty calls; Andy Devine is so appealing as Buck, the cracked-voice stagecoach driver, his character has become a western comic archetype, imitated by countless actors in the decades since. Most significantly, however, is Wayne, using his big break to show his range as an actor, and bringing to the screen a truly fascinating character who holds the viewer's attention whenever he appears. Other characters in *Stagecoach* vacillate between good and evil, but the Ringo Kid is the film's true hero, gentle and decent in the

"My friends just call me Ringo — nickname I had as a kid. Right name's Henry."

– the Ringo Kid (Wayne)

quieter moments, and fearless when it's time to fight.

The swagger and confidence Wayne brings to the Ringo Kid is pure acting. On the set, Wayne was insecure about working with established film actors. Adding to the pressure was his treatment from Ford, who insulted and degraded him in front of the cast and crew. Ford criticized Wayne's diction, his movement and his timing, and declared he was not working at his co-stars' level. Years later, Wayne claimed he was grateful for the abuse, saying it was Ford's deliberate method for sparking emotion in actors, forcing them to push through their self-doubts to give their best on-screen. It was also a technique, Wayne said, that was meant to attract sympathy from and solidarity with the other cast members, who might otherwise be stand-offish with the unknown actor on the set. The harassment motivated Wayne: In the small cabin he shared with stunt man Yakima Canutt during shooting, he rehearsed lines and movement every night, and showed up on the set each morning ready to deliver.

When *Stagecoach* was released in March 1939, critics were quick to dismiss it as a genre film and tended to praise the scenery more than the stellar cast and memorable performances. Frank S. Nugent, who later wrote the screenplay for the Ford-Wayne epic *The Searchers* (1956), wrote in his *New York Times* review of *Stagecoach* that "John Ford has swept aside ten years of artifice and talkie compromise and has made a motion picture that sings a song of camera." The cast, he added lightly, "have taken easily to their chores." In his review for *The New Yorker,* John McCarten wrote, "In *Stagecoach* the view is certainly something, and it hardly matters at all what goes on. The credit for the valuable things in this film unquestionably belongs to the cameramen..."

The public and the film industry, however, were not yet ready to dismiss westerns as a genre of the

Top: Hatfield, Samuel Peacock, and Lucy Mallory get their first look at the infamous Ringo Kid. Bottom: Monument Valley, Utah became a favorite shooting location for director John Ford after using it for *Stagecoach*.

The Ringo Kid settles for a seat on the stagecoach floor.

past. *Stagecoach* received seven Academy Award nominations, including Best Picture and Best Director; it won for Best Musical Score and Thomas Mitchell received the Best Supporting Actor prize for his performance as Doc. In a year with Technicolor extravaganzas like *Gone with the Wind* (1939) and *The Wizard of Oz* (1939), the film industry sent a message: they still loved westerns like *Stagecoach*, which is now regarded as a masterpiece of the genre.

"Well, I guess you can't break out of prison and into society in the same week."

— the Ringo Kid (Wayne) to Dallas (Claire Trevor)

Top: In a ramshackle desert oasis, the Ringo Kid lights a cigar as nighttime falls. Bottom: Though they've only just met on the stagecoach, the Ringo Kid is ready to settle down with Dallas.

DARK COMMAND (1940)

REPUBLIC PICTURES

DIRECTOR: RAOUL WALSH

SCREENPLAY: GROVER JONES, LIONEL HOUSER AND F. HUGH HERBERT

BASED ON THE NOVEL BY W.R. BURNETT

PRINCIPAL CAST: JOHN WAYNE (BOB SETON), CLAIRE TREVOR (MARY MCCLOUD), WALTER PIDGEON (WILLIAM "WILL" CANTRELL), ROY ROGERS (FLETCHER "FLETCH" MCCLOUD), GEORGE "GABBY" HAYES (DOC GRUNCH), PORTER HALL (ANGUS MCCLOUD) AND MARJORIE MAIN (MRS. CANTRELL)

The box office failure of *The Big Trail* (1930) set back the careers of John Wayne and Raoul Walsh for an entire decade. The vaunted director was saddled with one second-rate script after another, while Wayne was assigned to a spirit-crushing string of forgettable westerns. Finally, in 1939, John Ford rescued the actor and catapulted him to stardom in *Stagecoach,* and later that year *The Roaring Twenties* restored Walsh to the front rank. Capitalizing on their success, Republic Pictures reunited Wayne and Walsh on *Dark Command,* an action-packed, incident-filled historical drama set in Kansas in 1859, amid the rising tensions between North and South.

Wayne plays Bob Seton, an uneducated Texas cowboy traveling with a grizzled dentist pal named Doc Grunch (George "Gabby" Hayes). They set down stakes in Lawrence, where Seton falls for the banker's refined daughter, Mary McCloud (Claire Trevor). In short order, the underdog Seton is elected marshal, defeating dapper

Top: Hard-punching Bob Seton (Wayne) and tooth-pulling Doc Grunch (George "Gabby" Hayes) depart another town with money in their pockets. Bottom: Mary McCloud (Claire Trevor) rebukes her brother Fletch (Roy Rogers) and father Angus (Porter Hall) for arguing in the house.

Top: Bob Seton, with Doc Grunch and Fletch McCloud looking on, watches a Tennessee man being harassed before making his move. Bottom: Will Cantrell and Mary McCloud have a heart-to-heart chat.

schoolteacher William Cantrell (Walter Pidgeon), who was once Mary's beau. The bitter teacher, based on the notorious Confederate guerrilla William Quantrill, turns to brutal, opportunistic plunder after war breaks out, amassing a brigade of hooligans and terrorizing towns along the Kansas-Missouri border. The high-stakes battle between order and anarchy mirrors the escalating rivalry between Seton and Cantrell and propels *Dark Command* toward the climactic torching of Lawrence.

The penny-pinching Republic Pictures allotted an atypically generous budget for the film, and it's apparent in the spiffy costumes and well-populated crowd scenes. The major hitch was the strep throat that prevented Trevor from working for six weeks, and shut down the entire production. For his part, Walsh was pleased to discover that Wayne had acquired poise, presence, polish and power in the 10 years since *The Big Trail.* Indeed, *Dark Command* was an important film in Wayne's career not least because it proved he could act.

When the movie opened, the *New York Times* critic Bosley Crowther raved, "A lot of experience and talent has gone into the manufacture of Republic's *Dark Command*, and the consequence is the most rousing and colorful horse-opera that has gone thundering past this way since *Stagecoach.* If it's excitement you're looking for, you can go farther and do a lot worse." That was the public's verdict, also, and *Dark Command* became a big hit. The portrayal of Cantrell as a vindictive, amoral criminal — even his mother thinks he's the devil's spawn — rather than a Confederate sympathizer no doubt helped ticket sales in the South. Whatever the contributing factors, *Dark Command* established John Wayne as a box office draw in his own right.

SEVEN SINNERS (1940)

UNIVERSAL PICTURES

DIRECTOR: TAY GARNETT

SCREENPLAY: JOHN MEEHAN AND HARRY TUGEND

STORY: LADISLAS FODOR AND LÁSZLÓ VADNAY

PRINCIPAL CAST: JOHN WAYNE (LIEUTENANT DAN BRENT), MARLENE DIETRICH (BIJOU BLANCHE), ALBERT DEKKER (DR. MARTIN), BRODERICK CRAWFORD (EDWARD PATRICK "LITTLE NED" FINNEGAN), ANNA LEE (DOROTHY HENDERSON) AND MISCHA AUER (SASHA MENCKEN)

Initially, Tyrone Power was slated to star opposite Marlene Dietrich in *Seven Sinners*, but that changed when the movie queen laid eyes on John Wayne. According to director Tay Garnett:

Marlene had the choice of all her leading men. I decided not to mention Wayne to her, but simply to place him in the Universal commissary where she couldn't miss him. He stood between us and our tables as we walked in for lunch, chatting with a couple of actresses I had set up. Dietrich swept past him, then swiveled on her knees and looked him up and down as though he were a prime rib at Chasen's. As we sat down, she whispered right in my ear, "Daddy, buy me that!" I said, "Honey, it's settled. You got him." Then at a prearranged signal, Wayne came to the table. If you didn't know what was gonna happen, you'd be as blind as a pit pony. Their relationship got off like a fireworks display. They were crazy about each other.

Thus, thanks to Dietrich's pheromones, Wayne ended up co-starring as Lieutenant Dan Brent, the navy man

Top: "I'll give you a hand," Lieutenant Brent (Wayne) picks Bijou (Marlene Dietrich) up and lifts her over a herd of passing goats in their first meeting together. Bottom: "No, I don't want to make a scene, not for anything in the world," says Bijou to the menacing Antro (Oscar Homolka) before putting her cigarette out on his hand.

who falls for wanton seductress Bijou Blanche (Dietrich). As a cabaret performer at the Seven Sinners Café in the tropical South Sea isle of Boni Komba, Bijou excels at sending men into fits culminating in barroom brawls. Exiled from one exotic locale to another, she's used to high-stakes fun until she meets Dan, the affable lug who steals her heart. In one scene, she even dons navy drag and huskily warbles "The Man's in the Navy" as a befuddled Dan looks on. Of course, as expected, the naïve lieutenant and the worldly siren fall in love. Deciding to ditch the navy and settle down, Dan finds his domestic daydreams shattered when Bijou, thanks to a reality check from a friend ("A fellow can't get the navy out of his heart and blood"), comes tearfully to her senses and insists her beau return to uniform.

For Dietrich, then basking in the success of her comeback film, *Destry Rides Again* (1939), *Seven Sinners* proved that she was no longer "box office poison" in the eyes of the nation's motion picture exhibitors. For Wayne, this cheeky romantic action yarn helped burnish his rising star. Bijou's provocative seduction of Lieutenant Brent is particularly riveting, thanks to the contrast between big bad wolf Dietrich and sacrificial lamb Wayne. To heighten the effect, costume designer Irene dressed the Duke in virginal white, his uniform a series of straight, starched lines. By setting the stalwart naval officer adrift in the siren's bamboo hut as she struts about like a rare fowl draped in boas, feathers and veils, director Garnett keenly manages to win the earthy young Wayne an audience even in the presence of an established superstar.

Behind the scenes, art was imitating life. According to Wayne's daughter Aissa, her father's dalliance with Dietrich began when she invited him to her dressing room prior to the start of filming. As he stood idly by observing the star's lavish surroundings, Dietrich inquired, "I wonder what time it is?" Then, without provocation, she "lifted her skirt, revealing the world's most famous legs. Her upper thigh was circled by a black garter with a timepiece attached." She looked at it, inched closer to Wayne and said, "It's very early darling. We have plenty of time." After that, they were inseparable, with neither making any effort to hide the affair.

Although the Duke didn't like talking about the relationship, he did offer that "she was the most intriguing woman I'd ever known." He was equally candid during a 1979 interview with Barbara Walters when asked if he'd ever fallen in love with one of his co-stars: "Well, yeah...," he confided, "Marlene Dietrich."

Top: "You got me picking a wild orchid, that's a new low," Dan tells Bijou. Bottom: Honorable navy man, Lieutenant Brent comes to his senses and picks honor over love when he reports for duty in the bittersweet finale of *Seven Sinners*.

THE LONG VOYAGE HOME (1940)

UNITED ARTISTS

DIRECTOR: JOHN FORD

SCREENPLAY: DUDLEY NICHOLS

BASED ON FOUR PLAYS BY EUGENE O'NEILL

PRINCIPAL CAST: JOHN WAYNE (OLE OLSON), THOMAS MITCHELL (DRISCOLL), IAN HUNTER (SMITTY), BARRY FITZGERALD (COCKY), WILFRED LAWSON (CAPTAIN), JOHN QUALEN (AXEL), MILDRED NATWICK (FREDA), WARD BOND (YANK) AND ARTHUR SHIELDS (DONKEYMAN)

Based on four one-act plays by Eugene O'Neill, John Ford's *The Long Voyage Home* is set aboard the English cargo ship, the SS *Glencairn*, as it makes its way from the West Indies to England by way of Baltimore. Magnificently photographed by the brilliant cinematographer Gregg Toland, who would later collaborate with Orson Welles on *Citizen Kane* (1941), this character-driven film depicts the lives of the ship's crew with an artistry and depth of feeling that makes *The Long Voyage Home* one of Wayne's finest films.

In bringing O'Neill's *The Moon of the Caribees*, *In the Zone*, *Bound East for Cardiff*, and *The Long Voyage Home* to the screen, Ford and screenwriter Dudley Nichols changed the plays' World War I setting to World War II. Wayne portrays SS *Glencairn* crew member Ole Olson, an innocent Swede who only wants to earn enough money to return home to his family's small farm. Unlike his fellow seamen — a colorful group of grizzled, frequently drunken old salts — Olson is quiet and kind. When the

Top: Axel (John Qualen) and Olson (Wayne) aboard the merchant freighter *Glencairn*. Bottom: Wayne shows his range in the role of the Swedish sailor Olson.

ship must secretly take a cargo of munitions through a war zone, where the crew faces raging storms and enemy attacks, Olson gradually reveals the strength beneath his gentle façade.

The multifaceted role of Olson was challenging for Wayne, who practiced two hours a day to master the character's Swedish accent. He also had to hold his own opposite some of Hollywood's best character actors, including his *Stagecoach* (1939) co-stars Ward Bond, Thomas Mitchell and Arthur Shields, as well as Shield's older brother Barry Fitzgerald, a star of Ireland's Abbey Theatre. To his credit, Wayne easily rises to the challenge and gives a reserved but strikingly effective performance.

The Long Voyage Home was ecstatically received by critics and made many of the year's 10-best lists; the New York Film Critics Circle voted Ford its Best Director prize. Although the Motion Picture Academy overlooked Ford, *The Long Voyage Home* nevertheless received six Academy Award nominations, including Best Picture.

Critics also responded enthusiastically to Wayne's performance. The former star of cheap western serials was gradually proving himself to be a far more capable actor than previously imagined, as he so ably demonstrates in *The Long Voyage Home*.

Top: Olson, Axel and Driscoll prepare for an enemy attack. Bottom: Freda (Mildred Natwick) listens to Olson. Natwick was greatly impressed by Wayne's performance.

REAP THE WILD WIND (1942)

PARAMOUNT PICTURES

DIRECTOR: CECIL B. DEMILLE

SCREENPLAY: ALAN LE MAY, CHARLES BENNETT AND JESSE LASKY JR.

BASED ON THE SERIALIZED STORY BY THELMA L. STRABEL

PRINCIPAL CAST: JOHN WAYNE (CAPTAIN JACK STUART), RAY MILLAND (STEPHEN TOLLIVER), SUSAN HAYWARD (DRUSILLA ALSTON), PAULETTE GODDARD (LOXI CLAIBORNE), RAYMOND MASSEY (KING CUTLER), ROBERT PRESTON (DAN CUTLER), CHARLES BICKFORD (BULLY BROWN), LYNNE OVERMAN (CAPTAIN PHIL PHILPOTT) AND LOUISE BEAVERS (MAUM MARIA)

Although John Wayne got top billing in *Reap the Wild Wind* at the last minute, Ray Milland got the best part, with Wayne complaining he was there just to make Milland look like a "real man." Unhappy as he reportedly was, Wayne wouldn't have even had the part if Warner Bros. had been willing to loan out Errol Flynn to play Captain Jack Stuart, as director Cecil B. DeMille originally wanted. Wayne was worried that his fan base wouldn't accept him as the "heavy"; perhaps that's why he plays Stuart so ambivalently you don't even realize Stuart's the bad guy until the last act. But, as character actor Harry Carey Jr. observed, "By adding an element of deceit and double-dealing to his role, [the] Duke widened his emotional and intellectual growth as an actor."

The film, the second one DeMille shot in color, is not only notable for Wayne playing against type, but also for its subject matter. Premiering just three years after *Gone with the Wind* (1939) and playing while that Deep South spectacle was still in theaters, *Reap the Wild Wind*, as perhaps evident from its

Top: The Port of Key West looks suspiciously like Charleston or Savannah, one of many scenes in *Reap the Wild Wind* that evoke *Gone with the Wind* (1939). Bottom: Loxi (Paulette Goddard) shows her moxie and muscle when she stops a fight between Captain Jack Stuart (Wayne) and Steven Tolliver (Ray Milland) before it gets out of hand.

title, borrows liberally from its predecessor. Set in 1840, five years before Florida was admitted to the Union as a slave state, the film features a multitude of scenes depicting slaves and Southern society, and even opens with a *GWTW*-esque scene showing feisty Loxi (Paulette Goddard) in pantaloons. (Of course, not even *Gone with the Wind* could boast John Wayne in a diving suit battling a giant squid.)

Stuart and Loxi, the daughter of an old salvage captain, fall in love as she cares for him after his ship is wrecked on a reef. Although there's no hard evidence, everyone suspects that the pirates King Cutler (Raymond Massey) and his brother Dan (Robert Preston) are responsible for the wreck. Traveling to Key West to investigate is Stephen Tolliver (Milland), a young lawyer and the number two man for the shipping firm. He and Captain Stuart end up fighting over Loxi, fighting one another, and fighting the pirates who've been wrecking the ships.

Though reviews were mixed, *Reap the Wild Wind* became one of the Duke's biggest films of the 1940s. The special effects earned an Academy Award, and the cinematography, with backgrounds shot in Charleston and Key West, earned a nomination. And even though Wayne played the heavy in this exotic adventure, his fans and the critics still loved him. As the *New York Times* reviewer remarked, "John Wayne makes a rugged shipmaster [in this story] filled with sea storms, ship wrecks and gang fights, and peopled with picaresque characters, dashing gentlemen and ladies in crinoline."

Top: There's salvage to be had, but this time the dive is to search for something to prove Captain Stuart's guilt . . . or guarantee his innocence. Bottom: Because it was wartime and Japan occupied the chief rubber-producing countries, Paramount donated the film's giant rubber squid to the war effort after filming was completed.

THE SPOILERS (1942)

UNIVERSAL PICTURES

DIRECTOR: RAY ENRIGHT

SCREENPLAY: LAWRENCE HAZARD AND TOM REED

BASED ON THE NOVEL BY REX BEACH

PRINCIPAL CAST: JOHN WAYNE (ROY GLENNISTER), MARLENE DIETRICH (CHERRY MALOTTE), RANDOLPH SCOTT (ALEXANDER MCNAMARA), HARRY CAREY (AL DEXTRY), MARGARET LINDSAY (HELEN CHESTER), RICHARD BARTHELMESS (BRONCO KID FARRELL), MARIETTA CANTY (IDABELLE) AND SAMUEL S. HINDS (JUDGE HORACE STILLMAN)

The second of three films Wayne made with superstar and erstwhile lover Marlene Dietrich, *The Spoilers* sizzles with sexual tension when they're together on-screen, the steam fairly rising from their gazes, body language and banter. To be fair, Dietrich also generates plenty of sexual tension with Randolph Scott, playing the other man vying for her on-screen affections. In *their* scenes, however, they're acting.

This black-and-white barnburner is the fourth of five screen adaptations of Rex Beach's truth-based yarn set in rough-and-tumble Nome, Alaska, at the height of the gold rush in 1900. "The man's-man material has been somewhat softened to turn the story into a vehicle for Dietrich," Pauline Kael observed disapprovingly, but it had the unexpected benefit of showcasing a more playful and occasionally goofy John Wayne. Modeling one of Dietrich's character's feathered coats or sparring in blackface with her black maid (in a sequence in jarring bad taste today), Wayne is as relaxed and charming as he ever was on-screen.

Top: Alexander McNamara (Randolph Scott) has eyes for saloonkeeper Cherry Malotte (Marlene Dietrich) from the moment he meets her in the claims office. Bottom: Dex (Harry Carey) and Roy (Wayne) object to the judge's arbitrary and costly ruling on their mine claim.

Top: Roy calmly surprises Cherry and McNamara in her room. Bottom: Roy spells out the risks to other claimholders helping him take back his mine.

The Spoilers sets up two parallel competitions, for saloonkeeper Cherry Malotte (Dietrich) and the lucrative mines on the outskirts of the rowdy town. Roy Glennister (Wayne) and his trigger-happy older partner Dex (Harry Carey) operate one of the larger stakes, and Roy and Cherry have enjoyed each other's company for a while. The arrival of the law, in the form of gold commissioner Alexander McNamara (Randolph Scott) and Judge Horace Stillman (Samuel Hinds), along with the judge's daughter Helen (Margaret Lindsay), upends the business as well as the romantic arrangements.

While Dex is an old-school guy, prone to shooting first and dispensing with questions, Roy is a modern man willing to give the law a shake. When it turns out to be a nefarious claim-jumping scheme, Roy is quick to defend his holdings with a gun, a locomotive or his fists. Wayne delivers a typically strong performance as a fun-loving but upstanding man willing to fight for what he knows is right. As in most of his films, he isn't standing up just for his own interests but for the community's. Wayne isn't just a symbol of American iconoclasm and individualism, but of the western hero as visionary and nation-builder. Not that you'll hear Roy spouting such high-falutin talk.

There may not have been enough action for Kael's taste, but *The Spoilers* ends with a six-minute brawl between Glennister and McNamara that took 10 days to shoot. The epic fistfight begins in Cherry's room, tumbles into the hall and onto the balcony overlooking the saloon and casino, spills down the stairs and into the crowd of customers and, finally, onto the street. It remains one of the most famous fight scenes in cinema history — and reaffirmed Wayne's image as the most macho star of the era.

Flying Tigers (1942)

Republic Pictures

Director: David Miller

Screenplay: Kenneth Gamet and Barry Trivers

Principal Cast: John Wayne (Captain Jim "Pappy" Gordon), John Carroll (Woodrow "Woody" Jason), Anna Lee (Brooke Elliott), Paul Kelly (Hap Smith), Edmund MacDonald ("Blackie" Bales), Gordon Jones ("Alabama" Smith), Mae Clarke (Verna Bales) and Bill Shirley (Dale)

According to Wayne biographers Randy Roberts and James S. Olson, actor Aldo Ray reportedly said that director Howard Hawks should have sued the filmmakers responsible for *Flying Tigers*, given this film's blatant pilfering from Hawks' *Only Angels Have Wings* (1939). Indeed, the similarities are startling: the pilot with a past, the hotshot in it for himself, the new kid with "dead meat" writ all over him, the pilot grounded by medical problems (who valiantly flies anyway), and a leader called "Papa" or "Pappy." In fact, the only substantial differences between *Only Angels Have Wings* and Wayne's 1942 World War II action film are continent and context. Hawks set his film in South America with mail carriers; *Flying Tigers* takes place in Burma with American volunteers.

Truth is, the Flying Tigers — the volunteer group of American pilots in Burma led by retired U.S. Army Air Corps officer Claire Chennault, and named for the distinctive tiger shark face-paint on the front of their planes — were captivating enough without embellishment from unoriginal screenwriters. Two actual Tigers served

Top: Captain Jim "Pappy" Gordon (Wayne) in the cockpit of his Curtiss P-40. Bottom: "Pappy" and Brooke (Anna Lee) in an embrace. The film sent a clear message: Duty in wartime is more important than a relationship.

as consultants for the film, which became one of the highest-grossing pictures of 1942.

So why *didn't* Hawks sue? Well, it would have seemed downright unpatriotic, given that *Flying Tigers* was filmed only five months after Pearl Harbor; a war was on, and Hollywood had enlisted to help win it. That's surely why, as Wayne biographers note, "the film presented [noble] Chinese straight from the pages of Pearl S. Buck's *The Good Earth* and robotic Japanese fresh from hell." *Flying Tigers* is for the most part propaganda — it even includes Roosevelt's "infamy" speech in its entirety — and no one has ever taken to pro-American propaganda like the Duke. It's no surprise that *Variety* gleefully reported that in this film, "Wayne matches his best performance."

As to the film itself, *Flying Tigers'* heroine nurse Brooke Elliott (Anna Lee) is drawn to pilots who prove themselves selfless. For a while it's Captain Jim "Pappy" Gordon (Wayne), who's in charge of the volunteers training Chinese pilots and flying patrols as a defense against Japanese aggression. It seems hotshot pilot "Woody" Jason (John Carroll) doesn't stand a chance with her; at least not until he demonstrates some latent altruism by cheering up local Chinese war orphans and quietly giving his "ace" money to another pilot's widow. He thus wrangles a date with Nurse Elliott and leaves the base, missing his patrol. Taking his place is the young Hap Smith (Paul Kelly) — that's "Hap" as in hapless — officially grounded for a problem with his vision. Of course, as might be predicted, Hap comes to grief, setting the stage for one of the film's most memorable lines, delivered by Gordon when he sees Nurse Elliot with Woody: "I hope you two had a good time, 'cause Hap paid the check."

Top: "It's out of my hands now. None of these men will ever fly with you again," Pappy tells Blackie (Edmund MacDonald). Bottom: The Tigers' base may have looked like Burma, but the film was shot in Arizona, New Mexico, at the Curtiss-Wright Aircraft Co. in New York, and at Russell Ranch, California.

Wayne's first World War II film, *Flying Tigers* set the basic template for all the gung-ho, flag-waving combat films the Duke would make for the rest of his career.

PITTSBURGH (1942)

UNIVERSAL PICTURES

DIRECTOR: LEWIS SEILER

SCREENPLAY: KENNETH GAMET AND TOM REED

PRINCIPAL CAST: JOHN WAYNE (CHARLES "PITTSBURGH" MARKHAM),
RANDOLPH SCOTT (JOHN "CASH" EVANS), MARLENE DIETRICH
(JOSIE "HUNKY" WINTERS), FRANK CRAVEN (J. M. "DOC" POWERS),
LOUISE ALLBRITTON (SHANNON PRENTISS), SHEMP HOWARD
(SHORTY) AND SAMUEL S. HINDS (MORGAN PRENTISS)

Another western icon, Randolph Scott, joined Wayne to star in *Pittsburgh*, the story of two young coal miners who take on the steel industry. Marlene Dietrich shares the screen as love interest Josie "Hunky" Winters, a coal miner's daughter hankering for more out of life than just soot.

As an antihero of sorts, Wayne amply fills the film's title role with his portrayal of Charles "Pittsburgh" Markham, a bright young cad ascending the ladder of success while winning the heart of the determined Josie, whom he affectionately nicknames "Countess." Along for the ride is best friend John "Cash" Evans (Scott), whom Pittsburgh at first reveres but later reviles when Cash begins to question Pittsburgh's ethics.

Blinded by ambition, the calculating Pittsburgh dumps Josie and marries Shannon Prentiss (Louise Allbritton), the daughter of wealthy Morgan Prentiss (Samuel S. Hinds), the founder of the Prentiss Steel Company. Morgan's backing of the Markham and Evans Colliery catapults Pittsburgh and Cash into the big time where they soon

Top: "Look out!" Pittsburgh (Wayne) takes Josie (Marlene Dietrich) and Cash (Randolph Scott) on a joy ride. Bottom: "Hello Hunky, how's tricks?" Pittsburgh enjoys the power his newfound wealth provides him.

Top: Cash carries his own torch for Josie. Bottom: Wayne and Dietrich's steamy affair was on the verge of ending when they shot *Pittsburgh*.

find themselves at each other's throats. Pittsburgh, intoxicated by his newfound power, manipulates his wife while alienating Cash, who turns for comfort to the devastated Josie. Greed ultimately gets the better of Pittsburgh who, outfoxed by his father-in-law, finds himself ruined, his career essentially over.

Enter the Japanese. With the attack on Pearl Harbor and the start of World War II, Pittsburgh finally sees the error of his ways. He sets out to redeem himself by launching a patriotic business venture to supply the "arsenal of democracy" with steel for munitions.

One of the film's virtues is its unflinching look at the ambition and betrayals that ultimately lead to Pittsburgh's redemption. Thanks to the Duke's prodigious talent, Pittsburgh, even as his character becomes less sympathetic, still retains an appealing, childlike innocence. One notable sequence in the film is the riveting, no-holds-barred fight between Cash and Pittsburgh on some precariously high scaffolding. Slick with sweat, the two men hurl punches at one another as the suspense builds to a shocking twist.

Both Wayne and Scott exhibit plenty of chemistry here with the delicate Dietrich, which is no surprise in Wayne's case, since he and Dietrich were still an item off the set. Nevertheless, the affair that started during the filming of *Seven Sinners* (1940) was burning out, owing to the pair's opposing temperaments. Dietrich, determined to broaden the Duke's horizons, proffered the works of Proust and other European intellectuals, but Wayne balked; most likely, he had no time for such pursuits. In 1942, the Duke made an astonishing 5 films: *The Spoilers*, *In Old California* and *Flying Tigers* at the start of the year, *Reunion in France* followed by *Pittsburgh* toward the end (with the last two films both released in December). According to Wayne's daughter Aissa, her father was a "a slave to his energy" during this period in his career.

Ultimately, *Pittsburgh* proved a critical and financial failure — even in the thick of a global war, American audiences still agreed with Louis B. Mayer, that messages were the stuff of Western Union. *Pittsburgh* is by no means a bad film, but when propaganda supersedes entertainment, even the Duke can't quite save the day.

THE FIGHTING SEABEES (1944)

REPUBLIC PICTURES

DIRECTOR: EDWARD LUDWIG

SCREENPLAY: BORDEN CHASE

PRINCIPAL CAST: JOHN WAYNE (LIEUTENANT COMMANDER WEDGE DONOVAN), SUSAN HAYWARD (CONSTANCE CHESLEY), DENNIS O'KEEFE (LIEUTENANT COMMANDER ROBERT YARROW) AND WILLIAM FRAWLEY (EDDIE POWERS)

The Fighting Seabees is based on the real-life wartime construction battalions whose members were known as the Seabees. The Seabees were considered some of the hardest-working men in the struggle to win World War II. Once the Marines had landed in an area, the Seabees would follow to build just about anything the fighting men required, such as airstrips, barracks and oil tanks. They had a reputation for being men who were tough beyond the call of duty.

As The Fighting Seabees opens, World War II is raging, and Wedge Donovan (Wayne), head of a highly respected civilian construction company doing work for the navy, learns that some of his workers in the South Pacific have been killed by the Japanese because they were unable to defend themselves. Furious, Donovan complains to Lieutenant Commander Robert Yarrow (Dennis O'Keefe) about the regulation that prohibits civilian workers from bearing arms.

Yarrow and Donovan travel to Washington to persuade Captain Joyce (Addison Richard) to remedy the situation.

Top: "Why don't you dance with the guy that brung ya?" Constance Chesley (Susan Hayward) finds herself attracted to Lieutenant Commander Wedge Donovan (Wayne). Bottom: Lieutenant Commander Robert Yarrow (Dennis O'Keefe), Constance Chesley and Donovan at dinner.

Joyce agrees to establish construction battalions, but as this will subject Donovan's workers to many months of military training, he rejects the idea. Donavon and Yarrow leave for a South Pacific island where an airfield needs to be built. Meanwhile, Yarrow's girlfriend Constance Chesley (Susan Hayward), a war correspondent also assigned to the island, falls in love with Donovan.

When the Japanese attack the island, Donovan, believing his men have been abandoned, orders them to defend themselves with rifles. Unfortunately, this interferes with a trap that Yarrow's forces have set for the Japanese, resulting in heavy American casualties. A humbled Donovan finally agrees to have his men trained as Seabees. In the dangerous battles ahead, the quick-tempered Donovan's ability to follow orders will be tested and his deep feelings for Constance resolved.

The Fighting Seabees features a fine screenplay by Borden Chase and a well-chosen cast. Wayne even shows his footwork in a rare dance scene, when he performs the Jitterbug. Interestingly, George Reeves, the star of the 1950s-era television series *Superman,* was originally cast as Lieutenant Commander Yarrow, but the role went to Dennis O'Keefe when Reeves was drafted into the Army Air Corps.

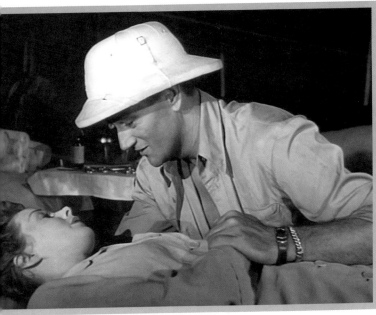

The film's battle scenes are exciting and well executed, and the score by Walter Scharf received an Academy Award nomination. Released in early 1944, *The Fighting Seabees* was a big hit and its rousing performance by Wayne struck a patriotic chord with wartime audiences.

Top: Yarrow and Constance share a poignant moment.
Bottom: Donovan comforts a wounded Constance.

BACK TO BATAAN (1945)

AN RKO RADIO PICTURES

DIRECTOR: EDWARD DMYTRYK

SCREENPLAY: BEN BARZMAN AND RICHARD H. LANDAU

STORY: AENEAS MACKENZIE AND WILLIAM GORDON

PRINCIPAL CAST: JOHN WAYNE (COLONEL JOSEPH MADDEN), ANTHONY QUINN (CAPTAIN ANDRES BONIFACIO), BEULAH BONDI (BERTHA BARNES), FELY FRANQUELLI (DALISAY DELGADO), RICHARD LOO (MAJOR HOSKO) AND PHILIP AHN (COLONEL COROKI)

John Wayne did not serve a day in the military. But by 1944 when shooting commenced on the World War II drama *Back to Bataan*, he was a well-established war hero on the big screen, at least, having appeared in *Flying Tigers* (1942), *Reunion in France* (1942) and *The Flying Seabees* (1944). *Back to Bataan* offered Wayne his juiciest wartime role as a soldier left behind enemy lines.

When American forces retreat from the Philippines in the wake of the Japanese invasion, Colonel Joseph Madden (Wayne) fades into the jungle with a ragtag group of soldiers and civilians. He and his men form the resistance, waging guerrilla war against the Japanese. What unfolds on-screen is an exhilarating tale of derring-do, the action divided between small-scale attacks and full-on combat that hits on all of the major facets of the Philippine occupation, including the Bataan Death March and liberation of the Cabatuan POW camp.

Not all of the drama in *Back to Bataan* took place in front of the cameras. When RKO producer Robert

Top: Wayne as Colonel Joseph Madden. Bottom: Madden (Wayne) and comrade Captain Andres Bonifacio (Anthony Quinn), a descendent of the legendary 19th century freedom fighter of the same name, share a quiet moment on Correigidor before hostilities begin.

Fellows ordered the movie into production, the Japanese still controlled the Philippines. The allied assault on the island began in October 1944, the month before filming got underway. With the situation still in flux, constant rewrites kept screenwriter Ben Barzman busy.

If that were not enough, in a presage of the postwar to come, a cold war broke out on set, pitting right-wing Wayne against left-wing Barzman and director Edward Dmytryk (a future member of the Hollywood Ten). Wayne sarcastically referred to Barzman as "our boy genius" and took every opportunity he could to take swipes at the writer. Barzman got his revenge by inventing difficult stunts for the star to perform, including one that involved jerking Wayne up with a crane before dropping him to make it look as if a shell had blown him into the air.

The stunt met with *Time*'s approval, the magazine calling it *Back to Bataan*'s "best shot," in a review that found the movie "straightforward, unsentimental, stirring." Bosley Crowther in the *New York Times* vehemently disagreed, lambasting the film as "a juvenile dramatization of significant history."

Back to Bataan met with box office success, but its flag-waving propaganda turned out to be wholly unnecessary. By the time Crowther's review appeared on September 13, 1945, World War II was over — if not for Wayne, who would fight on through half a dozen more films in the next 20 years.

Top: Sergeant Bernessa (J. Alex Havier) comes to Madden's aid after a mortar shell blows him out of a foxhole. Bottom: Madden dug in for battle to retake the Philippines.

THEY WERE EXPENDABLE (1945)

MGM

DIRECTOR: JOHN FORD

SCREENPLAY: FRANK WEAD

BASED ON THE BOOK BY WILLIAM L. WHITE

PRINCIPAL CAST: ROBERT MONTGOMERY (LIEUTENANT JOHN BRICKLEY), JOHN WAYNE (LIEUTENANT J. G. "RUSTY" RYAN), DONNA REED (LIEUTENANT SANDY DAVYSS), JACK HOLT (GENERAL MARTIN) AND WARD BOND ("BOATS" MULCAHEY)

When producer James McGuinness pitched the idea of filming William L. White's book *They Were Expendable* to renowned director John Ford, Ford initially turned him down. The Academy Award–winning director, who had served as a commander in the United States Navy, making documentaries like *The Battle of Midway* (1942), reportedly turned a deaf ear to McGuinness' impassioned description of White's book about the real-life wartime exploits of PT boat commander Lieutenant John Bulkeley. But once Ford met Bulkeley in person, the filmmaker was so impressed by the decorated hero's modesty that he changed his mind on the spot. The result is a classic film of heroism, directed with masterful restraint by Ford.

Top-billed Robert Montgomery plays Lieutenant John Brickley (the Bulkeley role), a PT boat squadron leader, with Wayne as Lieutenant J.G. "Rusty" Ryan, Brickley's right-hand man. In the aftermath of the attack on Pearl Harbor, they work together to convince Navy brass that

Top: Lieutenant "Rusty" Ryan (Wayne) assesses damage to the base following an attack. Bottom: Lieutenant John Brickley (Robert Montgomery) and Ryan are assigned a mission by Admiral Blackwell (Charles Trowbridge).

the maneuverability of PT boats will be a key issue in battles with the Japanese. When not taking on the Japanese forces in the waters off the Philippines, Ryan finds time to romance a brave nurse, Lieutenant Sandy Davyss (Donna Reed), but their romance ultimately takes a backseat to fighting the Japanese in the South Pacific.

They Were Expendable was filmed in Florida, which stood in effectively for the Philippines, Bataan and Corregidor. The crisp photography by Joseph H. August, who had military experience like Ford, gives *They Were Expendable* a documentary-like immediacy; the film's verisimilitude is further bolstered by the fact that Montgomery had served as a PT boat skipper.

They Were Expendable, with its powerful wartime themes of loyalty, sacrifice and stoic strength, is one of the most honest depictions of World War II made in the 1940s. The realism of the film's performances and situations extends to the spectacular battle scenes, which garnered Academy Award nominations for Special Effects and Sound.

According to Wayne biographers Randy Roberts and James Stuart Olson, reviewers were nearly unanimous in their praise for all aspects of the film, including Wayne's portrayal, yet 1945-era audiences were somewhat weary of war movies by the time *Expendable* premiered. Today, the film is highly regarded as one of Ford's most evocative — "a heroic poem" in the words of British filmmaker Lindsay Anderson.

Top: Ryan presides over the funeral of a fallen comrade. Bottom: Brickley and Ryan face the harsh realities of war in *They Were Expendable*.

ANGEL AND THE BADMAN (1947)

REPUBLIC PICTURES

DIRECTOR: JAMES EDWARD GRANT

SCREENPLAY: JAMES EDWARD GRANT

PRINCIPAL CAST: JOHN WAYNE (QUIRT EVANS), GAIL RUSSELL (PENELOPE WORTH), HARRY CAREY (TERRITORIAL MARSHAL WISTFUL MCCLINTOCK), BRUCE CABOT (LAREDO STEVENS), IRENE RICH (MRS. WORTH) AND LEE DIXON (RANDY MCCALL)

Quirt Evans (John Wayne) makes his entrance in *Angel and the Badman* wearing a black hat and waving his six-shooter in the air, fleeing a rival gang on horseback. On other occasions he draws his gun, or allows his reputation as a killer to save him the trouble, but — perhaps for the only time in Wayne's career — his character never pulls the trigger. In fact, this surprising and satisfying western plays for stretches like a romantic comedy. An expression of the pacifist ideal of beating swords into plowshares, *Angel and the Badman* neatly reflected the public mood following the terrible sacrifices of World War II.

Wounded and near death after that opening chase, Quirt is taken in and nursed by a Quaker family. They don't know of his evil ways and they don't care; their credo is to help anyone in trouble. The innocent daughter Penelope (Gail Russell) falls hard for the outlaw, and after he recovers Quirt sticks around to take a stab at going straight. Meanwhile, the local lawman bides his time, waiting for Quirt to commit a hanging offense.

Top: A just-awakened, ever-mistrustful Quirt Evans (Wayne) pulls a gun on his caregiver. Bottom: Temporarily domesticated, Quirt Evans takes a stroll to the barn with Penelope Worth (Gail Russell).

Angel and the Badman marked Wayne's first foray into producing, a job he took on in order to have more say about the kind of characters he played and the films he made. Wayne was no dilettante, though, and he devoted so much time and energy to his production company that his new bride, Esperanza, was beside herself. Instead of playing it safe and hiring an experienced director, Wayne took a chance and allowed veteran screenwriter James Edward Grant to make his debut behind the camera. Of course, with John Wayne's name on the marquee, the producer wasn't taking all that big a risk.

Whether it was his responsibility as a producer, his kindness to a co-star or his stalwart character, Wayne was keen to help the beautiful Gail Russell. Barely 22 at the time, the starlet had been thrust into movies in her late teens with little coaching or confidence, and had discovered that alcohol quelled her stage fright. Wayne spent so much time with her that Esperanza feared they were having an affair, a charge he denied up and down. In the ensuing years he funneled Russell occasional roles, but drinking took her career and her life. Russell died in 1961, a month shy of her 37th birthday.

Angel and the Badman received good reviews, but didn't strike box office gold. It wasn't the kind of hard-nosed shoot-'em-up that Wayne's audience preferred. That didn't faze Wayne, who produced another 18 movies, including several he didn't appear in, up through *The Alamo* (1960).

Top: Surprised in the middle of a tender moment with Penelope, Quirt pulls a gun on the territorial marshal (Harry Carey). Bottom: Before the climactic showdown, Quirt has a smoke to settle his nerves.

FORT APACHE (1948)

RKO RADIO PICTURES

DIRECTOR: JOHN FORD

SCREENPLAY: FRANK S. NUGENT

BASED ON THE SHORT STORY "MASSACRE" BY JAMES WARNER BELLAH

PRINCIPAL CAST: JOHN WAYNE (CAPTAIN KIRBY YORK), HENRY FONDA (LT. COLONEL OWEN THURSDAY), SHIRLEY TEMPLE (PHILADELPHIA THURSDAY), PEDRO ARMENDARIZ (SERGEANT BEAUFORT), WARD BOND (SERGEANT MAJOR MICHAEL O'ROURKE), GEORGE O'BRIEN (CAPTAIN SAM COLLINGWOOD), VICTOR MCLAGLEN (SERGEANT FESTUS MULCAHY) AND JOHN AGAR (SECOND LIEUTENANT MICHAEL "MICKEY" O'ROURKE)

After *They Were Expendable* (1945), John Ford wanted to make *The Quiet Man* with John Wayne, but the box office disappointment of Ford's *The Fugitive* (a 1947 film based on a Graham Greene novel) pushed that project into the future. For his next film Ford needed a guaranteed commercial success, and in the late 1940s and early '50s, nothing made the turnstiles move like a western . . . or John Wayne.

With a script from Frank S. Nugent — who would go on to write the screenplays for *3 Godfathers* (1948), *She Wore a Yellow Ribbon* (1949), *The Quiet Man* (1952), *The Searchers* (1956) and *Donovan's Reef* (1963) — Ford returned to starkly beautiful Monument Valley to film *Fort Apache*. For Wayne, it was his first time back since *Stagecoach* (1939), when entrepreneur and Native American advocate Harry Goulding had enticed Ford and his troupe to come to Goulding's Monument Valley Navajo Trading Post, adjacent to Navajo land just north of the Arizona-Utah border. In what quickly turned into a symbiotic relationship,

Top: Lieutenant Colonel Thursday and his daughter arrive by stagecoach. Bottom: Wayne as Captain Kirby York.

Goulding handed Ford an iconic location that would become synonymous with the director and the American West; Ford in turn bolstered the local economy, hiring Navajos at Screen Actors Guild wages and using his military connections to airlift hay and food into the area during a harsh winter the same year that *Fort Apache* was filmed.

Conditions were harsh for the stars too, by Hollywood standards. During *Stagecoach* everyone slept in tents, and while Goulding had added five small cabins for the director (who had his own) and stars (who had to double up), it was still Spartan. Every cabin had dirt floors, two cots, a kerosene heater, and a couple of dressers. Showers were a bucket of cold water, and there was no telephone. But the primitive conditions made it easy for the cast to get into their roles, and Wayne's co-star, Henry Fonda, likened it to summer camp.

Fort Apache is based on "Massacre," a short story by James Warner Bellah, who in turn drew inspiration from Custer's Last Stand. It's the first of three Ford films that would become known as his "Cavalry Trilogy," though it was never conceived that way. Ford simply found that he had a lot to say about the cavalry in such remote outposts, and it took him *Fort Apache, She Wore a Yellow Ribbon* (1949), and *Rio Grande* (1950) to have that conversation with filmgoers.

Monument Valley, Ford, and the Bellah-inspired trilogy were good for Wayne and his image. The

Top: The more rigid Lieutenant Colonel Thursday (Henry Fonda) berates the men for not dressing appropriately. Bottom: One of the breathtaking images of Monument Valley in *Fort Apache*.

Top: "The troop is ready, sir." Bottom: York and Thursday interrogate Meacham (Grant Withers), the Indian agent.

gigantic monolithic rock formations provided a natural counterpart to the Duke's larger-than-life screen persona, and Ford chose to shoot Wayne in a large number of up-angle shots, so that he too seemed to spring from the land in the same timeless, indestructible manner. Those shots also reinforced the film's themes and the character of Captain Kirby York, who's savvy about the rugged land and the ways of the Apaches. Wayne's character, York, stands in sharp contrast to Lieutenant Colonel Owen Thursday (Fonda), an easterner insistent on following rules and protocol to the letter; Thursday expects conformity and blind obedience from his men, though it clearly isn't appropriate for a western outpost. One seeks glory, and the other peace and fairness. It's a classic conflict of personalities and personal beliefs that brings out the best in both stars.

The tension begins with their very first meeting. "I bid you welcome, General Thursday," York says when the new commander interrupts a dance. "I'm not a general, Captain," the stiff and humorless Thursday corrects. York replies, "I'd remembered you as a general from the war, sir." And in that slight exchange, the audience is given to understand that the Lieutenant Colonel Thursday was demoted and sent to the most remote military post as a punishment. York has a past too, though one suspects his demotion had more to do with *not* following the rules rather than poor judgment. Then there's the scoundrel of an Indian agent, Silas Meacham (Grant Withers), who's been profiting by selling guns and liquor to the Apaches. As he's introduced to Thursday, Meacham quips, "Well, another exile in our wilderness." It's not long before York belts him for what he's done to disrupt the treaty that York negotiated with Cochise (Miguel Inclan) when he was commander. York is the moral compass for this film, and Wayne does an excellent job of playing a man who's bound by military honor to obey a superior officer whose thinking is decidedly inferior.

"Forward ho-o!" Following Thursday, the cavalry initiate their fateful action against Cochise and his warriors.

The supporting cast includes a number of distinguished character actors. Pedro Armendáriz, Ward Bond, Jack Pennick, Victor McLaglen, and Dick Foran play the sergeants who have fun at their dangerous jobs, while Anna Lee and Irene Rich give weight to those scenes when the cavalry rides out on a dangerous mission. And Ford good-luck charm Hank Worden appears as a southern recruit.

Westerns — and Ford's films are no exception — have been criticized for their racist or insensitive portrayals of Native Americans, but in *Fort Apache*, Wayne's character is an advocate for the Apache. If there's a villain, it's Meacham, who betrayed the Apaches and encouraged Diablo's band to leave the reservation. And while Lieutenant Colonel Thursday tricks the Apaches into returning to United States soil to initiate "Thursday's Charge," he comes across as far more noble and well-intentioned on-screen than in Bellah's short story. The presence of his daughter, Philadelphia (Shirley Temple), further humanizes him. It's this meticulous attention to character nuance and iconic imagery that makes *Fort Apache* complex, rather than the straightforward plot.

As the *New York Times* observed, John Wayne is "powerful" in *Fort Apache*. He's the plot lynchpin, too. In every scene, Wayne's character has a hand in trying to set things right and carries the message that the pioneer and cavalry spirit is a part of American resilience and fortitude. It's a role that Wayne pulls off with grace and restraint.

"Mickey! Get to Fort Grant. Tell 'em where we are. Tell 'em we may still be alive if they hurry. Move! . . . And MARRY that girl!"

— Captain Kirby York (Wayne)

Red River (1948)

United Artists

Director: Howard Hawks

Screenplay: Borden Chase and Charles Schnee

Based on the short story "The Chisholm Trail" by Borden Chase

Principal Cast: John Wayne (Tom Dunson), Montgomery Clift (Matt Garth), Walter Brennan (Nadine Groot), Joanne Dru (Tess Millay), Harry Carey Sr. (Mr. Melville), John Ireland (Cherry Valance), Coleen Gray (Fen), Harry Carey Jr. (Dan Latimer) and Noah Beery Jr. (Buster McGee)

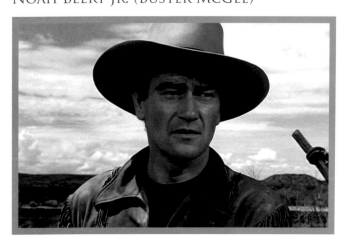

The independent men in Howard Hawks' muscular dramas lived and worked together, battling nature and one another, a model of professionalism. Their natures are one with the perfect western hero, which makes it all the more surprising that *Red River* was Hawks' first western. The collision of Hawks' typical themes with the epic sweep of the genre made for an explosive drama. It also provided a formidable showcase for the powerful talents of its star, John Wayne. After two decades in the business and nearly 10 years as a star, the Duke delivered his finest, most complex performance yet, establishing himself firmly as a screen personality of considerable force and influence.

Based on *Winchester '73* scribe Borden Chase's story "The Chisholm Trail," and adapted by Chase and Oscar winner Charles Schnee (*The Bad and the Beautiful,* 1953), *Red River* begins in 1851 as Tom Dunson (Wayne) and his partner Nadine Groot (Walter Brennan) head to Texas to start a cattle ranch. Over the next 15 years, the River

Top: Wayne gives one of his greatest performances as Tom Dunson in *Red River.* Bottom: "He'll do." Dunson nonchalantly informs Groot (Walter Brennan) that he'll adopt the young Matt Garth.

Red-D becomes an empire, but the Civil War nearly bankrupts Dunson, leaving him with no choice but to drive his ten thousand strong herd to marked. His foster son, Matthew Garth (Montgomery Clift), accompanies him on an arduous journey, tensions building between father and son over Dunson's callousness and merciless driving of his men. When Matt seizes control of the drive, the abandoned Dunson vows revenge.

Hawks originally wanted his *Sergeant York* (1941) star Gary Cooper to play Dunson, but Cooper was unwilling to inhabit such an unsympathetic character. Wayne had no such qualms. His only hesitation was that he just 39 years old and he wasn't sure he could play an "old man" like Dunson. "Duke, you're going to *be* one pretty soon, why don't you get some practice?" Hawks advised.

Wayne was appalled when Hawks had Brennan demonstrate how he should play the aged Dunson. "His idea of it was kinda shufflin' and totterin'. And mumblin'," Wayne explained. "I was supposed to be tough and hard and walk like that? Hell, I was thinkin' about those old cattle guys I knew when I was a kid around Lancaster and there wasn't one of them that didn't stand tall. I played Tom Dunson my own way, standin' tall. Oh yeah, Hawks and I had a few fights along the way, but he accepted me as an expert, which I was, and we did not have any more trouble."

Wayne's expertise extended to other aspects of the production. He proposed changes to the script and

Top: Though Wayne initially felt uncomfortable around Montgomery Clift, he slowly came to admire the young actor's dedication to his craft. Bottom: "Take 'em to Missouri, Matt." Dunson begins the 10,000 cattle drive to Missouri.

suggested increasing the original $1.5 million budget by more than 50 percent, insisting that Hawks hire real cowboys and professional stuntmen for greater authenticity. But he also saved the production money. The cattle cost $10 per head per day. Wayne showed Hawks how he could film the cattle drive to maximize the animals' on-screen numbers while using far fewer animals.

Clift was Hawks' third choice for Matthew after championship rodeo rider Casey Tibbs and *The Outlaw* (1943) star Jack Buetel. The Method-trained stage actor was a creative choice. The 26-year-old did not know how to fight or ride a horse and he had never been in a film.

Wayne was skeptical of the young actor, a feeling reinforced when Clift avoided eye contact with him the first time they met. "Christ, how does Howard expect that kid to stand up to me in a movie?" the exasperated star asked. "He can't even look me in the eye."

The two men never warmed to one another. "Clift is an arrogant little bastard," Wayne reported to a *Life* magazine editor. Clift was just as contemptuous of Wayne

Dunson and company come upon a dead colleague, killed in a cattle stampede.

"I was young and this was a challenge. It was the first time I felt like a real actor."

— Wayne on his performance as Tom Dunson in *Red River*

and Hawks, telling his friend Ben Bagley, "They laughed and drank and told dirty jokes and slapped each other on the back. They tried to draw me into their circle; I couldn't go along with them. The machismo thing repelled me because it seemed so forced and unnecessary."

On set, it was a different matter. Despite the director's assurance that Clift's intensity would translate well onto the screen, Wayne remained unconvinced until he saw the first rushes of the film. Wayne was so impressed with Clift's determination and hard work that he coached the rookie on how to throw credible movie punches and handle a gun. He also schooled Clift in film acting technique when, in a bid to break Clift of his stage mannerisms, Hawks had them improvise together.

The work paid off. Wayne and Clift are sensational together, perfectly complementing their respective characters and acting styles. Though it is clearly Wayne's film — Dunson dominates even when he is offscreen — Clift's internal, gentle sensitivity coexists as another form of masculine strength when played next to Wayne's external physical power and stoicism.

"Monumental in stature; sweeping in scope; and powerful in historical content...one of the screen's supreme examples of motion picture art and entertainment."

— *Variety*

Dunson vows to drive his cattle to Missouri.

The first and undisputedly the best of the five pictures that Wayne made with Hawks (the others being *Rio Bravo*, 1959; *Hatari!*, 1962; *El Dorado*, 1966; and *Rio Lobo*, 1970), it benefits from Russell Harlan's thrilling cinematography and Dimitri Tiomkin's strangely melancholic yet exultant music score. *Red River* is not only a superior western, it is a superior film — a marvelous blending of action, character development, vastness of scope, attention to intimate detail and visual lyricism.

The film was a critical and financial smash. "One of the best cowboy pictures ever made," raved the *New York Times'* Bosley Crowther. "The picture practically blows up with vitality and conviction," enthused *Time*. Wayne failed to secure a Best Actor Academy Award nomination, but the critics took notice. *Variety* called his performance "magnificent," while *Showmen's Trade Review* declared it to be "one of the most potent characterizations of which Hollywood can boast."

"No star in the history of film other than John Wayne could play this role in *Red River* and make it mean what it does and make the story mean what it does," wrote film historian Gerald Mast years later. In 1990, *Red River* was added to the National Film Registry. In 2008, it came in at number five of the 10 greatest westerns of all time in an American Film Institute poll. Decades after the film's release, *Red River* and Wayne's performance continue to resonate.

Dunson and Matt Garth about to cross the Red River.

"I never knew the big son of a bitch could act."

— Director John Ford after having seen Wayne's performance in *Red River*

"You should have let 'em kill me, 'cause I'm gonna kill you. I'll catch up with ya. I don't know when, but I'll catch up. Every time you turn around, expect to see me, 'cause one time you'll turn around and I'll be there. I'm gonna kill ya, Matt."

— Thomas Dunson (Wayne) to Matthew Garth (Montgomery Clift)

Top: Dunson refuses to acknowledge the hard work of his cattle drivers. Bottom: Tess Millay (Joanne Dru) tries to strike a bargain with Dunson.

3 GODFATHERS (1948)

MGM

DIRECTOR: JOHN FORD

SCREENPLAY: LAURENCE STALLINGS AND FRANK S. NUGENT

BASED ON THE NOVELLA BY PETER B. KYNE

PRINCIPAL CAST: JOHN WAYNE (ROBERT MARMADUKE HIGHTOWER), PEDRO ARMENDARIZ (PEDRO "PETE" FUERTE), HARRY CAREY JR. (WILLIAM "THE ABILENE KID" KEARNEY), WARD BOND ("BUCK" PERLEY SWEET), MAE MARSH (MRS. PERLEY SWEET) AND MILDRED NATWICK (THE MOTHER)

Peter B. Kyne's 1913 novella *The Three Godfathers* impressed director John Ford so much that he filmed it twice, first in 1919 as *Marked Men* and then again in 1948 as *3 Godfathers*. "As a film subject, it stood out as a classic with unlimited possibilities," Ford explained of this biblical allegory in which three bad men's actions mirror that of the Magi. Twenty-nine years after Harry Carey took center stage during the silent era, the spotlight passed to John Wayne as the leader of a criminal gang that stumbles unexpectedly on a path to redemption.

Outlaws Robert Hightower (Wayne), Pedro Fuerte (Pedro Armendariz), and William "The Abilene Kid" Kearney (Harry Carey Jr.) escape into the Arizona desert after robbing a bank. As a tense battle of wits plays between the thieves and the posse chasing them, a new wrinkle develops when the robbers come across a pregnant woman (Mildred Natwick). She dies during childbirth, but not before naming her unlikely saviors the baby's godfathers.

Ford dedicated *3 Godfathers* to the recently deceased Carey. The duo made more than 25 movies together, but

Top: Harry Carey Jr., Wayne and Pedro Armendariz as three outlaws who will soon have their lives turned completely around. Bottom: Silent screen star Mae Marsh with Ward Bond and Harry Carey Jr.

they had not worked together since making *The Prisoner of Shark Island* in 1936. A rift developed that Carey believed would heal only with his death. That prediction came true the day Carey died, when Ford informed his widow, Olive, that not only was he remaking *Marked Men* in her husband's honor, but he was casting their son in the movie, too.

Temperatures soared to 130 degrees at the film's Death Valley location, making shooting miserable for the stars. A windstorm scene that took days to complete was the worst of it, as two airplane propellers kicked up the sand, coating the actors. Wayne, at least, could relax a little. For once, he was not the recipient of Ford's browbeating and insults, as the director concentrated on hazing Carey Jr. "Ha, ha. He's just giving ya' the business. He's breaking you in," Wayne explained to the aggrieved young actor.

Wayne delivers a commanding performance, while Armendariz and Carey Jr. acquit themselves just as admirably. *3 Godfathers* was Ford's first color western and the Technicolor photography is stunning. Critics were impressed. "John Ford has filmed it so that the characters and gritty atmosphere slosh from the screen in great warm sluices of grandeur and emotion," raved the *New York Times'* Bosley Crowther, adding, "His unsurpassed talent for bringing upon the motion-picture screen the nature and the drama of the great West is in itself an art." Six decades later, *3 Godfathers* remains powerfully affecting.

Top: Wayne as outlaw Robert Hightower. Bottom: Jane Darwell and Ward Bond are part of the *3 Godfathers'* stellar ensemble.

WAKE OF THE RED WITCH (1948)

REPUBLIC PICTURES

DIRECTOR: EDWARD LUDWIG

SCREENPLAY: HARRY BROWN AND KENNETH GARNET

PRINCIPAL CAST: JOHN WAYNE (CAPTAIN RALLS), GAIL RUSSELL
(ANGELIQUE DESAIX), GIG YOUNG (SAM ROSEN), LUTHER ADLER
(MAYRANT SIDNEYE), ADELE MARA (TELEIA VAN SCHREEVEN), PAUL
FIX (RIPPER ARREZO), DENNIS HOEY (CAPTAIN MUNSEY) AND
HENRY DANIEL (JACQUES DESAIX)

In the long arc of John Wayne's career, the seafaring adventure *Wake of the Red Witch* is not an important film. Released the same year as Howard Hawks' *Red River* and John Ford's *Fort Apache* and *3 Godfathers*, it is a minor film in comparison. In Wayne's mind, though, it loomed large. He named his production company Batjac after the film's fictional trading company — and *Red Witch* itself later became a symbol of Wayne's battle with cancer. He would go for medical checkups or treatment, and wonder aloud to friends whether the *Red Witch* was lying in wait for him.

In this epic, fanciful adventure packed with revenge and adversarial interplay, Wayne plays Captain Ralls, who commands the *Red Witch*, a mighty trading vessel, until the day he inexplicably, but intentionally, runs it into a reef. Dangerous encounters with deadly sea creatures, a trove of pearls, gold bullion and two beautiful women, Angelique (Gail Russell) and Teleia (Adele Mara), all figure into action that unfolds in a series of flashbacks that eventually reveal why Ralls sank his own ship.

Top: The mighty sailing vessel, the *Red Witch*. Bottom: John Wayne as Captain Ralls.

Made by Wayne's home studio Republic Pictures, the $1.2 million shoot was one of the longest in the studio's history, lasting for more than three months. It was also a fraught production for the star. He spent so much time filming underwater that he developed an ear fungus. The production also exacerbated tensions in his marriage to second wife Esperanza Baur, when Wayne insisted that the studio cast his *Angel and the Badman* (1947) co-star Russell in the film. Wayne knew that Russell was a troubled alcoholic and his gesture was merely intended to boost a friend, but it enraged Esperanza, who was convinced that Wayne was romantically involved with his beautiful co-star.

Wayne delivers a vibrant, sporadically dark performance in *Wake of the Red Witch*, but critics of the era were split on this sprawling, uneven epic melodrama. "Story is a gripping account of deadly rivalry between two men," *Variety* enthused. The *New York Times'* Bosley Crowther disagreed, finding the sets and special effects obviously fake, and further grousing, "The ballast of reason and continuity is casually tossed overboard." The mixed reviews did not deter audiences. Two months after its December 1948 release, *Time* magazine reported that *Wake of the Red Witch* held the number two spot on the national box office chart.

Top: Luther Adler plays Mayrant Sidneye, a worthy adversary to John Wayne's Captain Ralls. Bottom: Angelique Desaix (Gail Russell) and Captain Ralls. Wayne insisted that Russell be hired as his co-star.

She Wore a Yellow Ribbon (1949)

RKO Radio Pictures

Director: John Ford

Screenplay: Frank S. Nugent and Laurence Stallings

Principal Cast: John Wayne (Captain Nathan Cutting Brittles), Joanne Dru (Olivia Dandridge), John Agar (Lieutenant Flint Cohill), Ben Johnson (Sergeant Tyree), Harry Carey Jr. (2nd Lieutenant Ross Pennell), Victor McLaglen (Top Sergeant Quincannon), Mildred Natwick (Abby Allshard), George O'Brien (Major Mac Allshard) and Arthur Shields (Dr. O'Laughlin)

Portraying a character 20 years his senior, Wayne, his hair streaked with gray, impressively proves in *She Wore a Yellow Ribbon* (1949) that his previous tour de force performance in *Red River* (1948) was no fluke. In director John Ford's ode to the vanishing Old West, Wayne delivers one of the finest screen portraits of his career as Captain Nathan C. Brittles, respected commander of the Seventh Cavalry.

The year is 1876. After the massacre at Little Big Horn, the robbing of a government-sponsored stagecoach and the murder of its driver, and the sudden, mysterious reappearance of the buffalo, Captain Brittles fears a war with the Cheyenne is at hand. About to retire in six days, he realizes his last mission must be driving the Cheyenne northward, out of harm's way.

Brittles is ordered by his commander, Major Mac Allshard (George O'Brien), to transport Mrs. Allshard (Mildred Natwick) and their niece Olivia (Joanne Dru) —

Top: A superlative example of Winton C. Hoch's Academy Award–winning cinematography. Bottom: Captain Nathan Brittles (Wayne) reading the casualty list from the Battle of Little Bighorn.

who wears a yellow ribbon in her hair — along with his Indian cavalry patrol from Fort Stark, where the cavalry is currently stationed. They are headed to Sudros Wells, a safer place for the women to charter a stagecoach east.

When Brittles and his battalion reach Sudros Wells, they discover the outpost has been brutally decimated by the Indians, and are forced to turn back to Fort Stark. Brittles deems his mission a failure and, despite his impending retirement, asks for a second chance to negotiate peace with the Indians.

She Wore a Yellow Ribbon was the second of John Ford's "Cavalry Trilogy" (bookended by *Fort Apache,* 1948, and *Rio Grande,* 1950) and the first and only one of the three to be shot in Technicolor. The director made subtle use of the Old West paintings of American artist Frederic Remington to give the picture an authentic look, rhythm and feel.

For Ford to photograph Monument Valley in color for the first time, he reunited with Winton C. Hoch (*3 Godfathers,* 1948) with whom he would subsequently work on *The Quiet Man* (1952), *Mr. Roberts* (1955) and *The Searchers* (1956). *She Wore a Yellow Ribbon's* twilight sequences would come to be regarded as some of film's finest Technicolor photography. Also justifiably celebrated is the famous thunderstorm sequence in which cavalrymen lead their horses through a rainstorm replete with dramatic bolts of lightning flashing intermittently in the purplish sky.

Top: Captain Brittles at his wife's grave. Bottom: Brittles and Sergeant Tyree (Ben Johnson) realize that the Arapaho Indians are moving in the same direction as C Troop Cavalry.

It's interesting to note that Ford undertook *She Wore a Yellow Ribbon* (and *Rio Grande* after that) to cash in on the success of *Fort Apache,* and that both films were specifically made to appeal to "kiddie-matinee" audiences. Despite the hurried shooting, the film, anchored and carried by Wayne's heroic performance, possesses surprising weight and distinction.

Wayne's Brittles is a tower of strength with a vulnerable core. His graveside conversations with his departed wife are extremely moving, as is the moment in which he reads the inscription "Lest We Forget" off a silver watch presented to him by his cavalry troop. Crediting much of his performance to Ford — "He gave me plenty of leeway" — the star did most of his own riding in the film, as well as a good portion of the stunt work. This is also the first film in which Wayne sports a mustache; he would do so again in *Rio Grande* (1950), *The Conqueror* (1956) and his final film, *The Shootist* (1976).

She Wore a Yellow Ribbon went into general release in October 1949 and became an instant hit. It deservedly won the Academy Award for Best Color Cinematography. Critical response was enthusiastic, with *New York Times* film critic

John Wayne's performance in *She Wore a Yellow Ribbon* should have netted him an Best Actor Academy Award nomination.

"You're an actor now."

— John Ford (message inscribed on a cake with one candle the director sent Wayne upon completion of *She Wore a Yellow Ribbon*)

Bosley Crowther leading the charge: "In this big Technicolored Western, Mr. Ford has superbly achieved a vast and composite illustration of all the legends of the frontier cavalryman." Both *Variety* and *The Hollywood Reporter* contended that the film set a new standard for westerns that would be hard to match.

To experience the film today is to acknowledge the usual Ford gender and ethnic stereotypes, of the Irish and Native Americans in particular, coupled with a contradictory mix of the overwrought (the drunken brawl near the end) and the sublime (the grandeur of the Western landscapes). *She Wore a Yellow Ribbon,* however, manages to transcend Ford's personal indulgences, thanks to its eloquent depiction of the universal themes of duty and devotion, unfolding as part of the inescapable cycle of life and death.

There was talk in Hollywood of Wayne as a possible Best Actor contender for *She Wore a Yellow Ribbon,* but he received his first Academy Award nomination for another film that year, *Sands of Iwo Jima* (1949). It seemed the years of hard work were finally paying for Wayne, one of the hardest-working and most prolific stars of the era. The onetime star of Poverty Row serials was now both a commercial and critical success.

"John Ford's New and Finest Picture of the Fighting Cavalry!"

— *She Wore a Yellow Ribbon* tagline

Cinematographer Winton C. Hoch's celebrated thunderstorm sequence.

SANDS OF IWO JIMA (1949)

REPUBLIC PICTURES

DIRECTOR: ALLAN DWAN

SCREENPLAY: HARRY BROWN AND JAMES EDWARD GRANT

PRINCIPAL CAST: JOHN WAYNE (SERGEANT JOHN M. STRYKER), JOHN AGAR (PRIVATE FIRST CLASS PETER CONWAY), ADELE MARA (ALLISON BROMLEY), FORREST TUCKER (PRIVATE FIRST CLASS AL THOMAS), WALLY CASSELL (PRIVATE FIRST CLASS BENNY REGAZZI), JAMES BROWN (PRIVATE FIRST CLASS CHARLIE BASS) AND JULIE BISHOP (MARY)

The end of World War II gave Americans the chance to take stock and look ahead, but it also marked the start of a long period of reflection about the conflict and the sacrifices made. Hollywood responded with a flurry of films that examined the war, from the homefront to the battlefield, in genres ranging from serious drama to musical comedy. Hundreds were made, but none tapped into American sentiment like *Sands of Iwo Jima*.

Directed by Allen Dwan, *Sands of Iwo Jima* depicts the historic World War II battles on Tarawa and Iwo Jima that culminated with a flag-raising and a famous photograph that captured the scene for posterity. At the center of the film is a marine platoon, introduced while they're enjoying the camaraderie and relative comfort of a New Zealand training camp in the months before they're shipped off to war. But breaking up the summer-camp joviality is the hard-nosed Sergeant John M. Stryker (John Wayne), who trains the men as if his life and theirs depended on it.

Top: Sergeant Stryker (Wayne) meets his men and lays down the law. Bottom: Private First Class Peter Conway (John Agar) meets his future wife, Allison (Adele Mara), at a soldiers' dance.

More martinet than mentor, Stryker delivers an almost constant barrage of verbal abuse, and if a man shows any resistance, Stryker doesn't hesitate to knock him flat.

The character has more than one dimension, however, as Wayne deftly reveals in small moments between raucous scenes. Stryker's devotion to the military cost him his marriage and young son, and the pain of that fact is a burden he relieves with drink whenever he gets the chance. His men are amazed to see Stryker, in town on liberty, staggering down the street incoherent and weak as a kitten. Stryker shows his vulnerability sober as well, when Mary (Julie Bishop), a local woman, shows him her baby daughter and he practically melts. He has a heart, it seems; he's just not willing to show it to his men.

Buoying Wayne's remarkable performance is John Agar, who plays Private First Class Peter Conway, the marine who may despise Stryker the most. Conway is frustrated and angry, with little respect for authority, but Stryker sees his potential and encourages him no matter how insolent Conway becomes. The bitter young man mellows just enough to court and marry big-eyed beauty Allison Bromley (Adele Mara), though even his romance seems tinged with rebellion. Surrounding Conway at camp and on the battlefield are a large group of talented young actors, including Wally Cassell as Private First Class Benny Regazzi, the camp cut-up, and Forrest Tucker as Private First Class Al Thomas, who finds out firsthand how bad it gets when Stryker blows his fuse.

Top: John Agar credited Wayne with teaching him how to act on film. Bottom: Stryker dances with Private "Sky" Choynski (Hal Fieberling) to teach him the rhythm of bayonet handling.

The battle scenes in *Sands of Iwo Jima* are thrilling to watch. Once they start, the only break from the excitement comes with the shots filmed on a Los Angeles soundstage, which are achingly unreal and a stark contrast from footage filmed outdoors with hundreds of extras plunging into battle punctuated by explosions. But the studio shots are far outweighed by the inclusion of real footage of American soldiers on Tarawa and Iwo Jima: grainy documentary film amazingly taken in the midst of actual combat. Even with state-of-the-art technology, no movie battle scene could match the intensity of the real thing in *Sands of Iwo Jima*.

Initially Wayne passed on making *Sands of Iwo Jima*. He didn't like the script or story, and even his friend Eddie Grainger, the film's associate producer, could not convince him to take the role. But Wayne had a change of heart when officials from the Marine Corps Commandants came to see him and implored him to take on the

In the heat of battle, Stryker orders his men to dig in and wait.

"Saddle up! Saddle up!"

— Sergeant John M. Stryker (Wayne) to his squad

66

Top: Stryker risks his life by lighting an explosive a few yards away from the enemy. Bottom: Actual footage of U.S. troops in battle was incorporated into *Sands of Iwo Jima.*

project. They saw it as a much-needed public relations opportunity and their best hope, at a time of shrinking military budgets, of preventing the Marine Corps from being eliminated. Wayne, who had never served in the military himself, was moved by their appeal and agreed to make the film, pending a thorough rewrite by his friend, the screenwriter James Grant.

The Marine Corps commitment to the making of *Sands of Iwo Jima* continued throughout production. For the boot camp and battle scenes, the filmmakers were given access to the Marine Corps Base Camp Pendleton near San Diego, a 196-square-mile property along the coast that could pass, with the right camera angles, for Pacific island beaches. For a price, the military also furnished equipment, from canteens to trucks, and servicemen to serve as extras in the large battle scenes. They had military advisors working on the film as well, though their notes on the script were not always heeded; a historically accurate account, in some cases, was deemed somewhat less exciting than the *Sands of Iwo Jima* script.

Sands of Iwo Jima quickly became a hit film after spectacular premieres in New York, Hollywood, Washington, D.C., and London. The Marine Corps embraced the film and the media attention it generated; Republic Pictures generated its own publicity by arranging for Wayne to have his hand and footprints enshrined at Hollywood's Grauman's Chinese Theater in a block of cement, mixed with black sand flown in from the real beach at Iwo Jima. The film became one of the year's top 10 moneymakers and garnered rave reviews for Wayne's performance, though the relentlessly patriotic tone left some reviewers cold. "It's loaded with the commercial ingredients of blazing action, scope and spectacle," *Variety* noted, "but it falls short of greatness because of its sentimental core and its superficial commentary on the war." The film industry was less concerned about the script's realism

On an ammunition run, Private First Class Al Thomas (Forrest Tucker) stops to enjoy a cup of coffee, with disastrous results.

and tone, and honored *Sands of Iwo Jima* with Academy Award nominations for screenplay, editing and sound. The Motion Picture Academy also nominated Wayne for Best Actor. Although he failed to win that year — Broderick Crawford received the golden statuette for *All the King's Men* (1949) — Wayne delivers one of his all-time greatest performances in *Sands of Iwo Jima*.

"Before I'm through with ya, you're gonna move like one man and think like one man. If you don't, you'll be dead."

— Sergeant John M. Stryker (Wayne) to his new rifle squad

"You gotta learn right and you gotta learn fast. And any man that doesn't wanna cooperate, I'll make him wish he hadn't been born."

— Sergeant John M. Stryker (Wayne)

Top: Stryker lets his men know they're risking their lives if they disobey him. Bottom: Stryker reflects on the military life with his right-hand man, Private First Class Charlie Bass (James Brown).

PART 2

1950-1959

OHN WAYNE: 1950-1959

resh off his success with *Sands of Iwo Jima* (1949), John Wayne began the 1950s with a hit film, *Rio Grande* (1950). The film's message of aggression, not diplomacy, toward one's enemies reflected Wayne's beliefs and resonated with American nces faced with the emerging Korean conflict. That same year, Wayne was named the popular star of 1950 by the *Motion Picture Herald*. It was a position he would hold in as well.

During this time, John Wayne had a contract with Republic Pictures, a studio he had been ciated with since 1935. He made films at other studios such as *Flying Leathernecks* (1951) Howard Hughes' RKO Pictures and *Operation Pacific* (1951) for Warner Bros., but his next r film, *The Quiet Man* (1952), was for Republic. *The Quiet Man* was John Ford's dream ct, but Herbert Yates, the head of Republic was quite vocal that it would fail. Despite the hat the film was a commercial and critical hit, Wayne refused to renew his contract with

WAYNE'S LEADING LADIES, 1950-1959

N BACALL
lley (1955)

etypal film noir femme fatale, evealed herself to be a fine ne and dramatic actress in 50s-era films as *How to Marry ire* (1953) and *Written on the 56)*. In the 1960s, Bacall all loned Hollywood for Broadway, e surprised fans and critics acclaimed, Tony Award–winning nce in *Applause*, the 1969 ased on *All About Eve (1950)*

ANGIE DICKINSON
Rio Bravo (1959)

Sexy and self-possessed, Dickinson is a talented actress who should have been a huge star. In a January 2008 *Vanity Fair* profile, writer Sam Kashner called her "the secret crush of generations of male moviegoers." Despite charismatic performances in *Rio Bravo* (1959), *The Chase* (1966) and *Point Blank* (1967), Dickinson found her greatest success on the small screen, starring in the 1970s-era NBC television series *Police Woman*.

SOPHIA LOREN
Legend of the Lost (1957)

Regally gorgeous yet warm and down-to-earth, Loren is far more than just one of the screen's all-time great bombshells: In 1961, she became the first actor in a foreign-language film to win the Academy Award for her shattering performance in *Two Women*. She later received a second Academy Award nomination for *Marriage Italian-Style* (1964). In contrast, she mainly provides "eye candy" in such Hollywood films as *Boy on a Dolphin* (1956), *It Happened in Naples* (1960) and *Fl*

Republic. He could not forgive Yates for his mistreatment of Ford — and he was infuriated that Yates would not support his own dream project, *The Alamo*.

Finished with Republic, Wayne teamed with Robert Fellows, a longtime colleague, to create an independent production company, Wayne-Fellows, in 1952. Together, they produced *Big Jim McLain* (1952), *Island in the Sky* (1953), *Hondo* (1953) and one of Wayne's most popular films, *The High and the Mighty* (1954).

However, as Wayne was joining forces with Fellows, his marriage to Esperanza "Chata" Baur was falling apart. After an ugly, public divorce proceeding that began in 1953, Wayne moved on to marry Pilar Pallete Weldy, a woman he had met on a 1952 location scouting trip in Peru. The following year, Robert Fellows sold his interest in Wayne-Fellows Productions to Wayne. The company was renamed, Batjac. It was supposed to be "Batjak" — a reference from Wayne's film, *Wake of the Red Witch* (1948) — but due to a clerical error, the last letter was mangled and Wayne let it stand.

MAUREEN O'HARA
Rio Grande (1950), *The Quiet Man* (1952) and *The Wings of Eagles* (1957)

The greatest of the Duke's leading ladies, O'Hara first caught the eye of Charles Laughton, who chose the Abbey Theater trained actress to co-star in two films: Alfred Hitchcock's *Jamaica Inn* (1939) and *The Hunchback of Notre Dame* (1939). Two years later, O'Hara starred in the classic *How Green Was My Valley* (1941), the first of several films she made with John Ford, who launched the Wayne-O'Hara screen partnership in *Rio Grande* (1950).

LANA TURNER
The Sea Chase (1955)

Hollywood's "Sweater Girl," Turner began her decades-spanning career at 16 in 1937, when *Hollywood Reporter* publisher William R. Wilkerson discovered her at the Top Hat Café. After playing bit parts and minor roles in a slew of MGM films, Turner became a star with *Ziegfield Girl* (1940), co-starring Judy Garland and Hedy Lamarr. The MGM glamour girl and tabloid staple later impressed critics with her performances in *The Postman Always Rings Twice* (1946) and *The Bad and the Beautiful* (1952).

NATALIE WOOD
The Searchers (1956)

The daughter of Russian immigrants, Wood made her screen debut at the age of 5 in *Happy Land* (1943), starring Don Ameche. She became a star with *Miracle on 34th Street* (1947), the Christmas-themed classic starring Maureen O'Hara. The rare child actor whose career didn't peak at the onset of puberty, Wood grew into a darkly beautiful and sensitive actress who gave Academy Award–nominated performances in *Rebel Without a Cause* (1955), *Splendor in the Grass* (1961) *and Love with a Proper Stranger* (1963).

In 1956, Wayne starred in the biggest flop of his career: *The Conqueror*, a laughably bad historical epic featuring a woefully miscast Wayne as Genghis Khan. Happily, he rebounded from that embarrassment with arguably his best film, John Ford's *The Searchers* (1956). Embraced by critics and audiences alike, this dark, morally complex epic was named the screen's greatest western in a 2008 American Film Institute poll.

Unfortunately, Wayne followed *The Searchers* with several underperforming films, including John Huston's costly historical epic *The Barbarian and the Geisha* (1958). Concerned for his career, he teamed up with the legendary director, Howard Hawks, to make the western *Rio Bravo* (1959). Critics were cool toward Hawks' film — it's now regarded as a classic — but the public flocked to *Rio Bravo*, which became the box office success Wayne needed.

Emboldened, Wayne finally embarked on this dream project, *The Alamo* (1960), as producer, director and star. The process was grueling, but Wayne was determined to bring forth his vision of a brave and righteous America. He would spend the following year trying to convince the rest of the world to share that vision.

"You know where you can put your contract. I'll never work here again."

— Wayne to Herbert Yates, head of Republic Pictures

Wayne in *Blood Alley* (1955).

Top: Wayne in *Island in the Sky* (1953), the second of his three films with director William A. Wellman. Bottom: Gunning for the enemy in *Operation Pacific* (1951).

RIO GRANDE (1950)

REPUBLIC PICTURES

DIRECTOR: JOHN FORD

SCREENPLAY: JAMES KEVIN MCGUINNESS

BASED ON THE SHORT STORY "MISSION WITH NO RECORD" BY JAMES WARNER BELLAH

PRINCIPAL CAST: JOHN WAYNE (LIEUTENANT COLONEL KIRBY YORKE), MAUREEN O'HARA (KATHLEEN YORKE), VICTOR MCLAGLEN (SERGEANT MAJOR TIMOTHY QUINCANNON), CLAUDE JARMAN JR. (TROOPER JEFF YORKE), J. CARROLL NAISH (GENERAL PHILLIP SHERIDAN) AND BEN JOHNSON (TROOPER TRAVIS TYREE)

Wayne's sixth film with director John Ford, *Rio Grande* marks the first time the superstar worked with the actress who became his all-time favorite leading lady: the beautiful, Irish-born Maureen O'Hara, who had previously starred in Ford's *How Green Was My Valley* (1941). The sparks fly between Wayne and O'Hara in this majestic and artfully realized western that brings Ford's "Cavalry Trilogy" to a riveting close.

A post–Civil War drama laden with romance and action, *Rio Grande* focuses on Lieutenant Colonel Kirby Yorke (John Wayne), a tough commanding officer whose cavalry troops are stationed at a remote fort near the Rio Grande's Mexican border. When Yorke returns to the fort with prisoners taken from a battle with the Apache, he learns that the Indians have been leading brutal raids from the Mexican side of the border, where his own troopers are forbidden to follow.

Top: Lieutenant Colonel Kirby Yorke (Wayne), unaware of the surprises in store for him, returns to camp at the beginning of *Rio Grande*. Bottom: Though the production was inexpensively shot, *Rio Grande* has the style and look of a much bigger, elegant and prestigious film.

While lecturing a group of new recruits about the dangers they'll soon face, Yorke discovers that his son Jeff (Claude Jarman Jr.), whom he hasn't seen in 15 years, is among the enlistees. Although he's underage, Jeff is determined to serve with honor under his father.

Another surprise arrives in the form of Yorke's estranged wife, Kathleen (O'Hara), who arrives to reclaim her son from the military. Since neither Yorke nor Jeff will give in to her demands, Kathleen decides to stay with the unit and help the other women in the camp. The escalating danger posed by the Apaches will soon challenge and test all of them. Threatened with a possible court-martial as he struggles to manage the situation, Yorke faces another, perhaps even greater challenge: rekindling his ties with Kathleen and Jeff.

Rio Grande was not planned to be part of Ford's "Cavalry Trilogy." The director originally wanted to make *The Quiet Man* (1952), but Republic Pictures owner Herbert J. Yates felt that property wasn't commercial enough. Yates agreed to finance *The Quiet Man* if Ford would first direct something commercial. So Ford put his dream project on the back burner to transform James Warner Bellah's short story "Mission with No Record" into *Rio Grande*.

The production was inexpensively shot on location (for *half* the cost of *Fort Apache*) in Moab, Utah, which resembled Monument Valley. Ford's desire was for

Top: "That's the policy and soldiers don't make policy, they merely carry it out." General Phillip Sheridan (J. Carroll Naish) with Yorke. Bottom: Yorke and Sergeant Major Quincannon (Victor McLaglen) discover that Yorke's son (Claude Jarman Jr.) has enlisted.

realism (the troopers uniforms were not washed during the monthlong shoot!) and spontaneity (his instructions to the stuntmen were vague). When Herbert Yates showed up unexpectedly one morning at 10:00 AM and asked Ford when he was going to start shooting, Ford replied: "When you get the hell off my set!" Yates complied and the shoot proceeded smoothly, with the notoriously irascible director in rare good humor.

Production credits are top-notch across the board. For a relatively low-budget film, *Rio Grande* has the look and feel of an epic. Victor Young's music score is sweeping and noble. Bert Glennon's photography has grandeur, pathos and intimacy, which the cinematographer graciously credited to Ford's "unlimited photographic sense."

The supporting cast is finely chosen. Claude Jarman Jr. is excellent as young Jeff. He is at once vulnerable, sensitive, tough and resilient. As expected, Ford regular Victor McLaglen steals scenes, while Johnson, J. Carroll Naish and Harry Carey Jr. provide solid support.

"Each one of you will have to do the work of ten men." Yorke rallies the troops.

"Put out of your mind any romantic ideas that it's a way of glory. It's a life of hardship and suffering and uncompromising devotion to your oath and your duty."

— Colonel Kirby Yorke (Wayne) to his son on requirements of military life

But the real magic of *Rio Grande* lies in Wayne's sizzling chemistry with O'Hara, who completely matches him with her indomitable will and strength of character. One of the screen's all-time great beauties, she holds her own against Wayne, who brings the necessary gravitas to the role of Yorke. The two stars would go on to make four more films together, most notably Ford's *The Quiet Man* (1952).

Both critics and audiences embraced *Rio Grande*, which became a big hit. Shortly after it premiered, legendary director Frank Capra cabled Ford: "Saw *Rio Grande*. It's great. After seeing the tripe that is being turned out today, it's a delightful pleasure to see a show made by the Old Master himself."

Rio Grande also solidified Wayne's position as a top box office draw. According to *The Motion Picture Herald*, he was now "Hollywood's most popular star."

"I think he is [a great soldier]. What makes soldiers great is hateful to me."

— Kathleen Yorke (Maureen O'Hara) on her husband, Kirby (Wayne)

One of the film's many action highlights is the exciting "Roman riding" scene with troopers Travis Tyree (Ben Johnson) and Daniel 'Sandy' Boone (Harry Carey Jr.).

OPERATION PACIFIC (1951)

WARNER BROS.

DIRECTOR: GEORGE WAGGNER

SCREENPLAY: GEORGE WAGGNER

PRINCIPAL CAST: JOHN WAYNE (LIEUTENANT COMMANDER DUKE E. GIFFORD), PATRICIA NEAL (LIEUTENANT MARY STUART), WARD BOND (COMMANDER JOHN T. "POP" PERRY), PHILIP CAREY (LIEUTENANT BOB PERRY), PAUL PICERNI (JONESY), WILLIAM CAMPBELL (THE TALKER), SCOTT FORBES (LIEUTENANT LARRY) AND MARTIN MILNER (ENS. CALDWELL)

Dedicated to the 3,500 U.S. submarine sailors lost during World War II and the entire "silent service," *Operation Pacific* is a gripping tribute to the bravery, teamwork and camaraderie of the men "sealed in steel," as the trailer colorfully described submarine crews. The dedication went beyond mere platitudes, as writer-director George Waggner mixed in actual battle footage to enhance the sense of verisimilitude and danger, and drew on two real-life incidents involving the late Commander Howard W. Gilmore of the USS *Growler* for the pivotal action centerpiece. As Lieutenant Commander Duke E. Gifford, John Wayne is in his element playing a trusted and respected leader of fighting men. The *Variety* reviewer concurred, noting, "Wayne, occasionally called upon to be over-heroic, still turns in a top-notch performance and has strong support right down the line."

One of the myriad pleasures of *Operation Pacific* is the relaxed, collegial professionalism that Wayne and Ward Bond (USS *Thunderfish* commander Commander John T. "Pop" Perry) bring to their scenes together. The longtime friends perform as peers, pals and equals to such a degree

Top: Lieutenant Commander Duke E. Gifford (Wayne) gathers information about the nearby Japanese destroyer. Bottom: Gifford shares a reflective cup of coffee with Commander John T. "Pop" Perry (Ward Bond).

Top: After four years, Gifford and his ex-wife, Lieutenant Mary Stuart (Patricia Neal), renew old acquaintances.
Bottom: Gifford "inspects" his inebriated seamen in jail after their run-in with the Pearl Harbor shore patrol.

that it's not always obvious who's the skipper and who's second in command. Of course, there's no doubt who was the number one box office draw in 1951, with Wayne's character the focus of the story from the tense opening rescue scene.

Operation Pacific alternates between the business of fighting the war at sea and the pleasures of R & R on Pearl Harbor, where Gifford's ex-wife, Mary Stuart (Patricia Neal), has been transferred. There's no bitterness between them; to the contrary, the plot is fueled to a substantial degree by the rekindling of their romance. Neal gives a vivacious performance as an independent woman still in love with a strong man, though she was not enamored of Wayne. She abhorred what she described as the star's bullying of the film's gay publicist and his battles with Waggner, although she recognized that Wayne was going through marital problems. But when Neal and Wayne reteamed several years later on another war picture set in Pearl Harbor, *In Harm's Way* (1965), she found the star had mellowed considerably.

Neal had her own romantic travails during *Operation Pacific*. Her substantially older lover, Gary Cooper, on the verge of separating from his wife with the intent of marrying Neal, was a frequent visitor to the set (supposedly to see his old friend, John Wayne, a fiction created to prevent gossip). The actress discovered she was pregnant during production and, at Cooper's behest, had an abortion. It was a painful episode for both of them, and Neal came to regret the decision in later years. Their affair ended in 1954, and Cooper reconciled with his wife.

The first film Wayne made under his new Warner Bros. contract, *Operation Pacific* netted the star a hefty salary by era standards: $150,000, plus 10 percent of the box office grosses. For the patriotic star, the United States Navy's approval of the film may have been even more gratifying than the money. *Operation Pacific* was regularly screened at naval bases around the world.

THE QUIET MAN (1952)

REPUBLIC PICTURES

DIRECTOR: JOHN FORD

SCREENPLAY: FRANK S. NUGENT

BASED ON THE SHORT STORY BY MAURICE WALSH

PRINCIPAL CAST: JOHN WAYNE (SEAN THORNTON), MAUREEN O'HARA (MARY KATE DANAHER), BARRY FITZGERALD (MICHALEEN OGE FLYNN), WARD BOND (FATHER PETER LONERGAN), VICTOR McLAGLEN (SQUIRE "RED" WILL DANAHER), AND MILDRED NATWICK (THE WIDOW SARAH TILLANE)

Perhaps the most personal film of John Ford's long and distinguished career, *The Quiet Man* is a masterfully crafted and emotionally satisfying work of popular art. A genuine labor of love for the director and his stars, this deceptively simple story of a turbulent romance in Ireland is a grandly entertaining showcase for John Wayne, who brings heartfelt conviction and quiet authority to *The Quiet Man*.

The star portrays Sean Thornton an American ex-boxer who's come to Innisfree, Ireland, to reconnect with his past, purchase the home he was born in and settle down to a peaceful and quiet life. But the village bully, Squire "Red" Will Danaher (Victor McLaglen, in a larger-than-life Oscar-nominated performance) also wants to acquire the house to be near the rich widow Sarah Tillane (Mildred Natwick). When Sean meets and falls in love with Danaher's tempestuous sister Mary Kate (Maureen O'Hara), all hell threatens to break loose. Sean's wooing of Kate and the wild events that follow make for boisterous good fun.

Top: Sean Thornton (Wayne) arrives in his birthplace, Innisfree, Ireland. Bottom: "Is that real? She couldn't be." Sean catches a glimpse of the beautiful Mary Kate Danaher.

Ford, who was of Irish descent (his birth name was Sean Aloysius O'Feeney) fell in love with the idea of turning *The Quiet Man* into a film when he first read the eponymous Maurice Walsh short story in the February 1933 issue of the *Saturday Evening Post*. For more than a decade *The Quiet Man* would ferment in the director's imagination, and despite his enthusiasm for the project, it would eventually take Ford nearly 20 years to bring it to the screen.

Ford shopped *The Quiet Man* around for years, unable to get it bankrolled; Twentieth Century Fox, Warner Bros. and RKO Radio Pictures all dismissed Ford's passion project as a stupid, silly Irish story that would never make a dime. Only after Ford signed a three-picture deal with Republic Pictures was he able to secure financing for *The Quiet Man* — *after* he made the box office hit *Rio Grande* for the "B movie" studio, run by penny-pinching Herbert J. Yates.

The Quiet Man was shot on location in a small, scenic village in County Mayo, Ireland, with some interiors photographed at Republic Studios in California. The budget was pricey by Republic standards: $1,750,000. Aside from Wayne and O'Hara, who had both made a "handshake deal" with Ford to star in the film in 1944, *The Quiet Man* features members of Ford's unofficial acting troupe, many of whom he considered personal friends: McLaglen, Natwick, Ward Bond and Barry Fitzgerald. Their presence did little to quell Ford's infamous temper; he fought with Yates and Wayne, who

Top: Sean kisses Mary Kate Danaher (Maureen O'Hara) for the first time. Bottom: "If anybody had told me six months ago that today I'd be in a graveyard in Innisfree with a girl like you I'm just about to kiss..."

was having a difficult time getting in character. Talking about *The Quiet Man* years later, Wayne said, "That was a goddamn hard script. For nine reels I was just playing the straight man to those wonderful characters, and that's really hard."

Happily, Wayne rose to the challenge of playing "the straight man." His performance in *The Quiet Man* is nothing short of a revelation. Looking, moving and speaking differently than in any of his previous film roles, Wayne exhibits qualities that he rarely displayed for audiences: a measured reticence and sensitivity. At the same time, Wayne's Sean Thornton is a physically imposing and emotionally direct character whose exchanges with O'Hara's fiery Mary Kate crackle with electricity and sexual tension. In fact, the intensity of these love scenes took a toll on the stars, especially O'Hara, who cracked a bone in her wrist when she had to punch Wayne in the jaw. In another scene, Wayne drags her across an Irish countryside covered in sheep manure; politically correct–minded

Sean and Mary Kate on their first day of courting.

"Wayne works well under Ford's direction, answering all demands of the vigorous, physical character."

— *Variety*

84

viewers may find such moments sexist, yet it's hard to resist this utterly charming and extraordinarily photographed romance, which Ford directs with obvious affection and great good humor.

Contrary to Herbert J. Yates' dire predictions, *The Quiet Man* was a resounding commercial and critical smash. It received a "thunderous ovation" at the Venice Film Festival, where it won the International Film Award. It was also nominated for seven Academy Awards, including Best Picture, and won Oscars for Best Cinematography (Winton C. Hoch and Archie Stout) and Best Director (John Ford's still unequaled fourth win in this category).

Though many Hollywood insiders felt that Wayne had given the best performance of his career to date, the Motion Picture Academy failed to nominate him for Best Actor. Snub notwithstanding, Wayne's performance in *The Quiet Man* is the most charming of his career.

Top: Sean and Mary Kate Danaher strike an unlikely wedding pose. Bottom: "There'll be no locks or bolts between us, Mary Kate... except those in your own mercenary little heart."

ISLAND IN THE SKY (1953)

WARNER BROS. PICTURES

DIRECTOR: WILLIAM A. WELLMAN

SCREENPLAY: ERNEST K. GANN

BASED ON THE NOVEL BY GANN

PRINCIPAL CAST: JOHN WAYNE (CAPTAIN DOOLEY), LLOYD NOLAN (CAPTAIN STUTZ), WALTER ABEL (COLONEL FULLER), JAMES ARNESS (MAC MCMULLAN), ANDY DEVINE (WILLIE MOON), HARRY CAREY JR. (RALPH HUNT), PAUL FIX (WALLY MILLER), DARRYL HICKMAN (SWANSON) AND CARL SWITZER (SONNY HOPPER)

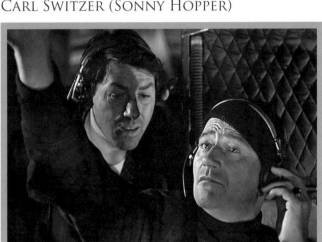

Critic Leonard Maltin calls *Island in the Sky* "the movie that slipped through the cracks" for the way it retreated into the mists of film history. Directed by William A. Wellman, it is an aerial adventure more focused on survival than daring maneuvers. As John Wayne films go, it is an anomaly — a luminous black-and-white drama in which the man of action is forced by circumstance into helpless waiting.

A civilian pilot attached to the military via the World War II–era Air Transport Command, Dooley (Wayne) is piloting a plane over Canada in subzero temperatures when the wings ice up and equipment begins to fail. Eventually, he has no choice but to bring the plane down on a frozen lake. Stranded in the arctic cold, Dooley can do little but try to convince his crew of five and himself that help is on the way. Their fellow fliers, including pilots Stutz (Lloyd Nolan), McMullen (James Arness), and Moon (Andy Devine), answer the rescue call, but are faced with the daunting task of searching through uncharted wilderness.

Top: Captain Dooley (Wayne) struggles to maintain control of his plane on a flight over Canada. Bottom: Co-pilot Frank Lovatt (Sean McClory) and Dooley discuss their prospects for survival as they explore their surroundings.

Ernest K. Gann, a veteran of the Air Transport Command, adapted *Island in the Sky*'s screenplay from his own fact-based novel and also served as the film's technical adviser. To advance the story's authenticity, Wellman secured a fleet of rare DC-3s and shot the all-important wilderness survival scenes on frozen Donner Lake, California, in the dead of winter. The film was made under the auspices of Wayne-Fellows, Wayne's production company, and co-star Darryl Hickman remembered Wayne as a hands-on producer: "I remember being out on location and I remember John Wayne helping them carry cameras places."

"I had the feeling that this was one of the chances that he had to combine his action hero self with his acting self," Hickman added. Reviews of the time keyed in on the former quality with *Time* magazine remarking, "John Wayne plays perfectly the lean and leathery hero that has made him a top box office attraction for years." But 55 years after the film's release, the *Onion*'s Keith Phipps saw it differently, writing, "Wayne's image was larger than life, but passing himself off as an everyman was one of his best tricks." Wayne is certainly at his most vulnerable in *Island in the Sky*, as he lets fear peek from behind the courage in a performance that emphasizes both a character's and an actor's grace.

Top: Dooley scans the horizon for signs of a rescue plane. Bottom: Co-pilot Sonny Hopper (Carl Switzer) and Captain Stutz (Lloyd Nolan) navigate by the stars in hopes of finding their downed friends.

HONDO (1953)

WARNER BROS. PICTURES

DIRECTOR: JOHN FARROW

SCREENPLAY: JAMES EDWARD GRANT

BASED ON THE SHORT STORY "THE GIFT OF COCHISE" BY LOUIS L'AMOUR

PRINCIPAL CAST: JOHN WAYNE (HONDO LANE), GERALDINE PAGE (ANGIE LOWE), WARD BOND (BUFFALO BAKER), MICHAEL PATE (VITTORIO), LEE AAKER (JOHNNY LOWE) AND LEO GORDON (ED LOWE)

In the opening frames of *Hondo*, John Wayne strides out of the desert landscape and into close-up, a literal and symbolic image of the Old West: rugged and dangerous. It's not a grand entrance, but an entrance that becomes grand for its utter simplicity — the kind of entrance only Wayne could make. It encapsulates perfectly why he became and remains a legend. Based on a short story by Louis L'Amour, *Hondo* remains a classic of the western genre and showcases Wayne in one of his best roles.

Wayne plays Hondo Lane, a Cavalry dispatcher who encounters lone homesteader Angie Lowe (Geraldine Page) and her son Johnny (Lee Aaker) after he loses his horse while escaping Apache Indians. Though Angie tells him that her husband is out herding wayward cattle and is due home soon, Lane quickly surmises that Angie has been alone for some time and that her husband is not coming back. As the Apaches are about to wage war, Hondo encourages Angie to leave the homestead, but

Top: Wayne as Hondo Lane in John Farrow's adaptation of a Louis L'Amour short story. Bottom: Wayne reportedly wasn't a fan of newcomer Geraldine Page's Method acting, but Page got the last laugh, earning an Academy Award nomination for her performance.

Angie is determined to stay, convinced that she can continue to maintain a peaceful relationship with the tribe. The threat of war soon proves real, however, and Angie realizes that if she wants to maintain peace, she will have to marry an Apache brave. Instead, she tells them that Hondo is her husband; the Cavalry dispatcher must then decide between his love for Angie and his own blood ties to the tribe.

Wayne intended to serve only as a producer for his company Batjac, but took the title role when Glenn Ford turned it down, citing an unpleasant experience working with director John Farrow in *Plunder of the Sun* (1953). It's hard to imagine anyone but Wayne playing the part. Originally filmed to cash in on the popularity of 3-D, the film was converted to a flat version when the 3-D craze fizzled shortly before the film's release. The images hold up beautifully, and the foreground compositions only intensify Wayne's imposing persona.

Acclaimed stage actress Geraldine Page made her film debut in *Hondo* and turned in an Academy Award–nominated performance, one that still holds up today. The film is also noteworthy for its somewhat more sympathetic and complex portrayal of Native Americans, who had often been portrayed in narrow, stereotypical fashion in earlier films.

Hondo remains a rich film experience and a must-see for any fan of the classic western drama.

Top: Hondo fends off an ambush by Apache Indians.
Bottom: Wayne took the title role after Glenn Ford rejected it.

THE HIGH AND THE MIGHTY (1954)

WARNER BROS. PICTURES

DIRECTOR: WILLIAM A. WELLMAN

SCREENPLAY: ERNEST K. GANN

BASED ON THE NOVEL BY GANN

PRINCIPAL CAST: JOHN WAYNE (DAN ROMAN), CLAIRE TREVOR (MAY HOIST), LARAINE DAY (LYDIA RICE), ROBERT STACK (JOHN SULLIVAN), JAN STERLING (SALLY MCKEE), PHIL HARRIS (ED JOSEPH), ROBERT NEWTON (GUSTAVE PARDEE) AND DAVID BRIAN (KEN CHILDS)

A forerunner of the 1970s-era airplane disaster films, *The High and the Mighty* was one of John Wayne's most successful movies in the 1950s. Based on Ernest K. Gann's bestseller, William A. Wellman's film closely follows the novel, introducing its cast of characters as they check in at the Honolulu airport for a flight to San Francisco. In all, 22 people board the DC-4, including a young couple (Karen Sharpe and John Smith) returning from their honeymoon, a disillusioned scientist (Paul Kelly), an aging broad (Claire Trevor), an insecure beauty (Jan Sterling) and a doting husband (Phil Harris). Flying the plane is Captain John Sullivan (Robert Stack), an experienced pilot who is nevertheless starting to crack under pressure.

Wayne, who produced *The High and the Mighty* with his partner Robert Fellows, portrays co-pilot Dan Roman, a role originally intended for Spencer Tracy. Haunted by a tragic accident in his past, Roman must act decisively when one of the plane's engines catches fire over the Pacific. Although the fire is quickly extinguished, the damage to

Top: Co-pilot Dan Roman (Wayne) reports for duty.
Bottom: Crew members Wheeler (William Campbell), Wilby (Wally Brown), Roman and Captain Sullivan (Robert Stack) react to engine trouble.

the plane is severe. Facing a life-and-death situation, the crew and the passengers pull together in the hopes that they can reach San Francisco safely.

Roman explains the dire situation to the passengers.

The second of two aviation-themed films Wayne made with Wellman — they had previously worked together on *Island in the Sky* (1953) — *The High and the Mighty* was filmed in Cinemascope on cramped quarters on the Samuel Goldywn lot. Wayne initially planned just to produce the film, but when Tracy rejected Wellman's offer to play Roman, Wayne stepped in to provide box office insurance. In fact, several A-list stars, including Joan Crawford, Ginger Rogers and Barbara Stanwyck, also turned down roles in *The High and the Mighty*, presumably because they didn't want to share screen time as members of an ensemble cast.

A hit with audiences and the Motion Picture Academy, *The High and the Mighty* received six Academy Award nominations; only composer Dimitri Tiomkin emerged victorious, taking home the golden statuette for Best Music Score.

Admittedly, time has not been very kind to *The High and the Mighty*, which unfolds like a glossy soap opera in the skies, complete with extended flashbacks. Rising above the kitsch is Wayne, who's steadfast in a film that *New York Times'* critic Bosley Crowther aptly describes as "spitting fire, tossing propellers and strewing emotional wreckage all over the place."

THE SEA CHASE (1955)

WARNER BROS. PICTURES

DIRECTOR: JOHN FARROW

SCREENPLAY: JAMES WARNER BELLAH AND JOHN TWIST

BASED ON THE NOVEL BY ANDREW GEER

PRINCIPAL CAST: JOHN WAYNE (CAPTAIN KARL EHRLICH), LANA TURNER (ELSA KELLER), DAVID FARRAR (COMMANDER JEFFREY NAPIER), LYLE BETTGER (CHIEF OFFICER KIRCHNER), TAB HUNTER (CADET WESSER), RICHARD DAVALOS (CADET STEMME), JAMES ARNESS (SCHLIETER) AND JOHN QUALEN (CHIEF ENGINEER SCHMITT)

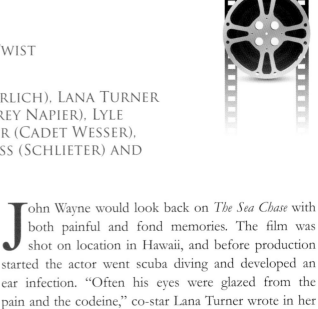

John Wayne would look back on *The Sea Chase* with both painful and fond memories. The film was shot on location in Hawaii, and before production started the actor went scuba diving and developed an ear infection. "Often his eyes were glazed from the pain and the codeine," co-star Lana Turner wrote in her autobiography. "His ear was so swollen that for a number of days they could shoot only one side of his face. Between takes he'd go to his bunk and lie down, suffering quietly." The pleasant memories involved the resolution of Wayne's marital situation at the end of the shoot.

The Sea Chase centers on a German sea captain, Karl Ehrlich (Wayne), whose outspoken anti-Nazi sentiments have cost him his command and landed him at the helm of a rundown tramp steamer. The *Ergenstrasse* is anchored in Sydney's harbor when World War II breaks out, but Captain Ehrlich resolves to get his boat and men home. He is asked to transport Elsa Keller (Lana Turner), a German agent and adventuress running out on her fiancé, British naval Commander

Top: German spy Elsa Keller (Lana Turner) works her wiles on Captain Ehrlich (Wayne). Bottom: Ehrlich and Elsa lay their cards on the table during a quiet stretch in the *Ergenstrasse*'s voyage.

Napier (David Farrar). Under Ehrlich's ingenious and inspiring leadership, the *Ergenstrasse* eludes Allied ships, but a brutal act by the ship's first mate launches Commander Napier in dogged pursuit. Meanwhile, a romance develops between Ehrlich and Keller. It requires a major suspension of disbelief to accept all-American John Wayne as a German, but he wisely refrains from affecting an accent and Ehrlich is cut from the same mold as countless Wayne heroes: he's principled, self-assured and action-oriented. The main challenge director John Farrow and his screenwriters faced was crafting the film's ending; no Wayne fans wanted to see their idol die, but it wouldn't do to let a German officer escape with the whole war ahead. Wayne easily gets us rooting for him, even in his unlikely interplay with Turner. As the *Variety* reviewer observed, "Wayne, as a he-man type, seems a little embarrassed in delivering some of the boy-girl talk that occurs as he, at first hating, gradually comes to love the spy aboard his freighter."

Although newcomer Tab Hunter was disappointed by his tiny, dispensable role in *The Sea Chase*, Wayne's generosity impressed the young Warner Bros. contract player. "You have a nice quality when you act," the Duke told him. "But I was like you at your age — had to learn to keep broader in certain scenes, not play down emotionally." Wayne even gave Hunter his navy jacket to wear on-camera as a good-luck token.

The Sea Chase is an enjoyable and picaresque film, though Wayne remembered it best for what happened after shooting wrapped October 30, 1954. Two days later, he got a call from Los Angeles saying his divorce from Esperanza Baur was official. That very day Wayne married Pilar Weldy, and they were together for the next 17 years.

Top: Ehrlich single-handedly quells the crew's resistance to smashing the lifeboats into fuel for the ship's engines. Bottom: Ehrlich and Elsa study the charts and weigh their options on a stormy night in the North Sea.

BLOOD ALLEY (1955)

WARNER BROS. PICTURES

DIRECTOR: WILLIAM A. WELLMAN

SCREENPLAY: A.S. FLEISCHMAN

PRINCIPAL CAST: JOHN WAYNE (TOM WILDER), LAUREN BACALL (CATHY GRAINGER), PAUL FIX (MR. TSO), JOY KIM (SUSU), BERRY KROGER (OLD FENG), MIKE MAZURKI (BIG HAN) AND ANITA EKBERG (WEI LONG)

John Wayne made several anti-Communist pictures throughout his decades-spanning film career, among them *Big Jim McLain* (1952) and *The Green Berets* (1968). But *Blood Alley*, his third film with director William Wellman, is arguably the best of the lot.

Wayne plays Tom Wilder, a sailor in the Merchant Marine who has been imprisoned in a Communist Chinese jail for two years. He's finally released, thanks to a bribe from 180 Chinese villagers to prison officials. The villagers need an experienced sea pilot to navigate a ferry through the 300-mile Formosa Strait, known as "Blood Alley," so they can escape to freedom in Hong Kong.

Accompanying Wilder and the villagers are an American woman, Cathy Grainger (Lauren Bacall), the village elders led by Mr. Tso (Paul Fix), his American-educated nephew Tack (Henry Nakamura) and Wilder's imaginary girlfriend "Baby," a composite of all the girls

Top: "A trip down Bloody Alley in a ferry boat is no Sunday excursion," Captain Tom Wilder (Wayne) informs Cathy Grainger (Lauren Bacall). Bottom: Wayne took over the role of Wilder after Robert Mitchum clashed with *Blood Alley* director William A. Wellman.

he has ever known. The journey, rocked by dramatic setbacks, is fraught with suspense, peril and murder.

Blood Alley was the first film from Batjac, Wayne's new independent production company. According to Randy Roberts and James Stuart Olson's biography *John Wayne American*, Robert Mitchum was originally cast at Wilder, but he and Wellman clashed so bitterly that Wellman told Wayne, "It's either Mitchum or me. Either you star or I'm out of the picture." Faced with Wellman's ultimatum, Wayne reluctantly left the side of his new wife, Pilar, to join the cast and crew on location in San Rafael, California.

When *Blood Alley* premiered in October 1955, it failed to make much of an impression with critics. *Newsweek*'s reviewer put it succinctly: "Good ship, shallow draft." Yet the $2.5 million production has its virtues, ranging from Alfred Ybarra's atmospheric production design to Roy Webb's dramatic score. Best of all, there's Wayne in top form, the very embodiment of can-do resolve and heroism in the face of an unrelenting threat. Ignoring *Blood Alley*'s mediocre reviews, the public turned out to see their idol in all his larger-than-life glory.

Top: Wilder fleeing Communist agents on the road to Hong Kong. Bottom: "The bleeding heart of China. You can pin one on my sleeve, baby."

THE SEARCHERS (1956)

WARNER BROS. PICTURES

DIRECTOR: JOHN FORD

SCREENPLAY: FRANK S. NUGENT

BASED ON THE NOVEL BY ALAN LEMAY

PRINCIPAL CAST: JOHN WAYNE (ETHAN EDWARDS), JEFFREY HUNTER (MARTIN PAWLEY), VERA MILES (LAURIE JORGENSEN), WARD BOND (REVEREND CAPTAIN SAMUEL JOHNSTON CLAYTON), NATALIE WOOD (DEBBIE EDWARDS) AND HENRY BRANDON (CHIEF CICATRICE, "SCAR")

After playing roles as diverse as an airline pilot and a Mongol warrior, John Wayne reunited with longtime friend and mentor John Ford in the mid-1950s to create a new type of western: one that stripped away the archetypal cowboy veneer to reveal the flawed humanity beneath the dust and leather. *The Searchers* has typically exciting action sequences and breathtaking scenery, but it has surprises too, and not all of them as cheerful as the perfect blue skies stretching across the screen in cinematographer Winston C. Hoch's poetically rendered compositions. On the surface, Wayne's character in this adaptation of Alan LeMay's novel may recall the men he played in Ford's *3 Godfathers* (1948) and *Rio Grande* (1950), but *The Searchers'* Ethan Edwards is unlike any protagonist in Wayne's entire filmography.

The Searchers opens on a high desert homestead, with Ethan Edwards (Wayne) returning to the comfort of his brother's family after years of fighting in the Confederate

Top: The leader of the posse, Reverend Clayton (Ward Bond), finishes his breakfast while Ethan Edwards (Wayne) says good-bye to his sister-in-law Martha (Dorothy Jordan) for the last time. Bottom: Finding a slaughtered steer, Ethan realizes they've been tricked by Comanche warriors.

army. Almost immediately, he's called back into action when the Reverend Captain Sam Clayton (Ward Bond) assembles a posse to go after cattle rustlers he believes have moved into the area. But when cattle are discovered slaughtered, Edwards and the posse, including his brother's adopted son, Martin Pawley (Jeffrey Hunter), realize that the Comanche tribe has tricked them into leaving their homes unprotected. Edwards and Pawley return to find the other adult family members killed, and the young girls abducted. Thus begins Edwards and Pawley's obsessive quest to find the girls — a search that will span years and exact a heavy toll on both men.

Over time, however, Edward's heroic intentions are eclipsed by his relentless, all-consuming hatred of the Comanche tribe. He loses his bearings morally and mentally; the film's unblinking depiction of Edwards as a tortured soul, all but forsaking his humanity to realize his goal, gives *The Searchers* the emotional heft and complexity of tragedy. His comrades in the posse are shocked when he calmly shoots at a half-buried Comanche corpse. Nor does Edwards have any compunction about using Pawley as bait for an ambush. After five long years of searching for his niece Debbie (Natalie Wood), Edwards comes to the conclusion that she must now be more Comanche than white and therefore should be killed.

Wayne dominates every scene of *The Searchers*, but he doesn't overpower his co-stars, especially Jeffrey Hunter, who excels as the eager and excitable Pawley.

Top: Ethan Edwards explains the Comanche attack plan to the gathered Texas Rangers. Bottom: Comanche warriors position themselves on the ridge to attack the Texas Rangers below.

Longtime Wayne crony Ward Bond steals scenes with his engaging performance as the Reverend Sam Clayton; he's pious at the breakfast table but murderous on the trail, always with his arrogant head held high. Newcomer Vera Miles shines in her brief but important role as the farm girl in love with Pawley, as does teenaged Natalie Wood as Debbie. The other standout in *The Searchers'* supporting cast is Hank Worden as the addlepated Mose Harper, who's kindly and gentle but handy with a gun. Wayne's son Patrick also makes an appearance, as a by-the-books calvary officer ready for action though barely old enough for a shave.

The Searchers premiered just three weeks after the debacle of *The Conqueror* (1956), the laughably awful Genghis Khan biopic that had earned Wayne the worst reviews of his entire career. The timing of the releases, as well as the unanimously negative reviews for *The Conqueror,* had a direct effect on the reception of the new Ford-Wayne collaboration. Perhaps they were still reeling from the camp spectacle of a miscast Wayne as the Mongol warrior, but many critics initially failed to recognize *The Searchers'* greatness. In his short-sighted

"I still got my saber, Reverend. Didn't turn it into no plowshare, neither."

— Ethan Edwards (Wayne) to Reverend Captain Samuel Johnston Clayton (Ward Bond)

Ethan Edwards tells his young counterparts Brad Jorgensen (Harry Carey Jr.) and Martin Pawley (Jeffrey Hunter) that they'll be taking orders from him.

(and short — three lines total!) *New Yorker* review, John McCarten described Ford's film as Wayne and company "tearing around Texas." McCarten's review fairly dripped condescension as he tersely concluded, "The film has to do with the search for a couple of maidens some nasty Comanches have abducted shortly after the Civil War, and it certainly contains plenty of action."

Over time appreciation for *The Searchers* grew considerably among fans of the western genre, including many film critics and scholars. Andrew Sarris of *The Village Voice* wrote in 1969 that "Wayne's performances in *The Searchers, Wings of Eagles* (1957) and *The Man Who Shot Liberty Valance* (1962) are among the most full-bodied and large-souled creations of the cinema." Film societies came to embrace *The Searchers*, not just as a great western, but as a masterpiece of cinema. In *Sight and Sound*'s 1992 international critics' poll, *The Searchers* was ranked the fifth greatest film of all time. And in 2008, the American Film Institute named Ford's film the greatest western ever made. In *A Biographical Dictionary of Film*, David Thomson hails *The Searchers* as "a very moving and mysterious film … filled with disturbing, half-buried thought of race and failure."

Reverend Clayton and Ethan Edwards fight off the first wave of the Comanche attack.

"I'm givin' the orders, hear? I'm givin' the orders. And you'll follow 'em or we're splittin' up right here and now."

— Ethan Edwards (Wayne) to Martin Pawley (Jeffrey Hunter)

Wayne understood how special *The Searchers* was and didn't wait until critical opinion shifted before he called the film a success. He asserted publicly that the part of Ethan Edwards was the best role he ever had, and that his performance in the film was the best of his career — a belief shared by many critics. In fact, the beauty of Wayne's performance lies in his ability to suggest the deep-seeded loneliness and isolation that's lurking beneath Edwards' hostile, unrepentantly racist façade. He is a man forever on the outside looking in, as the film's classic final shot so poignantly conveys.

Six years after its release, Wayne paid tribute to *The Searchers* in a more private way. With his favorite character in mind, he named his newborn son John Ethan Wayne.

Monument Valley, was a favorite shooting location for director John Ford.

"We'll find 'em in the end, I promise you. We'll find 'em. Sure as the turning of the Earth."

— Ethan Edwards (Wayne) to Martin Pawley (Jeffrey Hunter)

Top: By the first snowfall, only Ethan Edwards and Martin Pawley are still on the trail of the Comanche. Bottom: Laurie Jorgensen (Vera Miles) is thrilled to have Martin Pawley back again, if only for a day.

LEGEND OF THE LOST (1957)

UNITED ARTISTS

DIRECTOR: HENRY HATHAWAY

SCREENPLAY: ROBERT PRESNELL JR. AND BEN HECHT

PRINCIPAL CAST: JOHN WAYNE (JOE JANUARY), SOPHIA LOREN (DITA), ROSANNO BRAZZI (PAUL BONNARD) AND KURT KASZNAR (PREFECT DUKAS)

Three people battle for survival in the inhospitable Sahara Desert in director Henry Hathaway's *Legend of the Lost*. That struggle was reflected behind the scenes during the making of this adventure tale, as calamities visited the set. John Wayne severely injured his foot in a fall during filming. His co-star Sophia Loren nearly died when the gas heater asphyxiated her while she slept. In addition, conditions were rough for the entire cast and crew. With only tents or rough lodgings, no phone or radio, minimal plumbing, and only one flush toilet, the isolated Libyan location 400 miles from civilization offered the stars a taste of the life-threatening dangers their characters face in *Legend of the Lost*.

Paul Bonnard (Rosanno Brazzi) arrives in Timbuktu seeking a guide for a mysterious trip into the Sahara. The local prefect recommends Joe January (Wayne), an American residing in the village. Bonnard also befriends petty thief and prostitute Dita (Loren) after she steals his watch. As January and Bonnard set off on their arduous

Top: *Legend of the Lost* was filmed in Libya under physically grueling conditions. Bottom: Joe January (Wayne) and Paul Bonnard (Rosanno Brazzi) disagree as to their actual location and heading in the Sahara Desert.

journey, Dita follows. She wants to stay with them, and January allows it, despite his misgivings.

As the unlikely trio make their way across the Sahara, Bonnard finally reveals that he is searching for a lost city said to contain a vast treasure; he intends to use the windfall to finance a refuge for the sick and needy. Dita soon comes between the two men, adding another layer of danger as they comb the desert for the treasure.

The tension on *Legend of the Lost* was not solely between the characters. Wayne and Brazzi got on well, while Brazzi and Loren got on even better, as they enjoyed an affair despite her engagement to producer Carlo Ponti. But Wayne was cool and distant toward Loren, never warming to the Italian screen goddess.

Jack Cardiff's evocative Technirama desert cinematography is superlative, while Ben Hecht's screenplay brings out interesting character development and insightful observations about human nature. *Legend of the Lost* is an unusual film; its subtle spirituality, philosophy and journey-of-the-soul mysticism lend it a unique distinction. Unfortunately, these qualities went virtually unnoticed when the film was released. It was "authentic Hollywood hokum," in *Time*'s view, and the magazine was not alone in dismissing the movie. But its narrative depth, excellent production values, and Wayne's charismatic performance belie that assessment of this minor but nonetheless noteworthy film.

Top: January helps solve a mystery that's long puzzled Bonnard. Bottom: The striking and sensual Dita (Sophia Loren) makes quite an impression on Bonnard.

RIO BRAVO (1959)

WARNER BROS. PICTURES

DIRECTOR: HOWARD HAWKS

SCREENPLAY: JULES FURTHMAN AND LEIGH BRACKETT

BASED ON THE SHORT STORY BY B.H. MCCAMPBELL

PRINCIPAL CAST: JOHN WAYNE (SHERIFF JOHN T. CHANCE), DEAN MARTIN (DUDE), RICKY NELSON (COLORADO), ANGIE DICKINSON (FEATHERS), WALTER BRENNAN (STUMPY) AND WARD BOND (PAT WHEELER)

John Wayne was concerned during the making of *Rio Bravo*. The drama revolves around his co-star Dean Martin's character, a drunk whose desperation sets calamity in motion. "Hey, Martin gets all the fireworks, doesn't he? What do I do?" Wayne asked director Howard Hawks. What the actor did was completely inhabit a true Hawksian hero, Sheriff John T. Chance, who's courageous, loyal, competent, uncompromising and humorous. It is, wrote filmmaker Peter Bogdanovich, "among Wayne's most likeable performances."

An evening that begins with Joe Burdette (Claude Akins) toying with Dude (Martin) in a saloon ends with Burdette locked up for murder. Chance has no doubt that the man's rancher brother Nathan (John Russell) will stop at nothing to spring his sibling. It is a sticky situation. Chance has only two deputies, elderly Stumpy (Walter Brennan) and the shaky Dude. He wouldn't mind having gunslinger Colorado (Ricky Nelson) on his team, but he understands the teen's reluctance to enter someone else's battle. Nathan Burdette's hired guns are not the only

Top: Wayne as Sheriff John T. Chance. Bottom: The cowboy crooners Colorado (Ricky Nelson) and Dude (Dean Martin) take a ride.

challenges confronting Chance. Unwilling to abandon his friend to the bottle, he becomes Dude's keeper. Then there is the erotic charge he gets from new friend Feathers (Angie Dickinson). Loaded six-shooters do not scare the bashful lawman nearly as much as Feathers' loaded flirtation.

The world that Chance and his friends inhabit is quintessentially Hawksian, a universe where men nonchalantly go about their daily business even as danger lurks, accepting the possibility of violent death without complaint. What Hawks and Wayne faced was not nearly so fraught, but they both had something to prove. Hawks had not made a film since his CinemaScope epic *Land of the Pharaohs* (1955) had landed with a thud at the box office.

As for Wayne, *The Searchers* (1956) was the last western he'd made, and none of the four movies he'd starred in since had been particularly successful. It was time to return to the genre that had served his career so well. Who better to partner with than Hawks, the director who had coaxed a career-best performance out of Wayne the decade before in *Red River* (1948)? Martin might have *Rio Bravo*'s showier role, but Chance is the anchoring center around which all the other characters revolve. When Wayne asked his plaintive, "What do I do?" Hawks had an answer ready.

"It was a story of friendship," the director explained. "I said, 'What would happen to you if your best friend

Top: Feathers (Angie Dickinson) and her flirtatious smile charm Chance. Bottom: During a visit to his jailed brother Joe (Claude Akins), Nathan Burdette (John Russell) confronts Chance.

had been a drunk and he was trying to come back — wouldn't you watch him?' He said, 'OK, I know what to do.'"

Fred Zinnemann's acclaimed western *High Noon* (1952) served as the inspiration for *Rio Bravo*. Made at the height of the Cold War, *High Noon* has often been interpreted as a Red Scare parable, since it depicts a frontier marshal who cannot recruit any townspeople to help him fight off a murderous enemy. The politically conservative Wayne was appalled by Zinnemann's film, saying, "It's the most un-American thing I've seen in my entire life."

Hawks loathed *High Noon*, as well, but for a different reason. He simply despised its hero lawman's behavior. "I said [*High Noon*] was phony. The fellow's supposed to be good, supposed to be good with a gun. He runs around like a wet chicken trying to get people to help. Eventually, his Quaker wife saves his guts. I said, 'That's ridiculous!' The man wasn't a professional," Hawks complained. The attitude Chance strikes in *Rio Bravo* is exactly the opposite and the movie's *raison d'etre*. Urged by his friend Pat Wheeler (Ward Bond) to ask the townsfolk for help, he rejects the suggestion. This is a fight for the pros; there is no place in it for amateurs.

"He is so adorable in it. He's very cuddly kind of in this. I can't think of another John Wayne movie where he is that way."

— Angie Dickinson on *Rio Bravo*

Stumpy (Walter Brennan) stands guard from a strategic position. Opposite page: Colorado picks a crucial moment to join Chance's fight against Nathan Burdette's hired guns.

In contrast to *High Noon*, much of *Rio Bravo* takes place in the dark, heightening the tension. Chance and Dude patrol silently through the border town's narrow streets, aware of the peril that might leap out of the gloom at any moment. Inside the claustrophobic jail, the circumstances are even dicier. The men are proverbial sitting ducks under siege there, but they are determined to hold their position. Despite the long odds, they retain the cool confidence of professionals. Death might be looming, but they keep the atmosphere light, with the rambunctious Stumpy providing comic relief and Dude and Colorado entertaining their pals with song as Chance affectionately watches.

When *Rio Bravo* opened in March 1959, the public liked it, as it went on to earn $5.8 million at the box office, but it did not receive the acclaim that greeted *High Noon*. There were no Academy Award nominations. The reviews were good, but not ecstatic. A.H. Weiler in the *New York Times* praised Wayne's "satisfyingly laconic" performance and admitted that *Rio Bravo* was an above-average western but sniffed, "Chances are that a wide-awake viewer will not be particularly startled by its random fireworks." *Variety* called it "a big, brawling western," approvingly noting that it "gets off to one of the fastest slam-bang openings on record."

"Quite often, certain protagonists and movie stars, it is their glory that they do not change. John Wayne so often is that movie persona. He's strong at the beginning, he's strong in the middle, and he's strong at the end. And he responds to the circumstances, but he supplies a great moral force."

— Director Walter Hill on *Rio Bravo*'s continuing appeal

Over the years, those early mixed reviews have become more and more of an anomaly as *Rio Bravo*'s stock has continued to rise. French New Wave pioneer Jean-Luc Godard found it "a work of extraordinary psychological insight and aesthetic perception." "It's American filmmaking at its finest — clean, clear, and direct — and it's also the most optimistic masterpiece on film, valiantly shoring fragments against human ruin," wrote the *Chicago Reader*'s Dave Kehr. Director John Carpenter insists that *Rio Bravo* is "the ultimate western. It's got everything in it." In fact, Hawks' film so moved him that he placed his own spin on it with his urban thriller *Assault on Precinct 13* (1976).

Wayne and Hawks went on to make three more films together, including two westerns, *El Dorado* (1966) and Hawks' uneven final film *Rio Lobo* (1970) which were kind of unofficial sequels to *Rio Bravo*. It was a partnership the director cherished. "When you have someone as good as Duke around," Hawks said, "[it's] awfully easy to do good scenes."

Chance and his men enjoy a moment of peace before the fireworks begin.

"Suppose I got 'em? What did I have, some well-meaning amateurs, most of them worried about their wives and kids. Burdette has thirty or forty men, all professional. The only thing they're worried about is earning their pay. No, all we'd be doing is givin' more targets to shoot at."

— Sheriff John T. Chance (Wayne) explaining why he won't be deputizing any citizens

Top: Surrounded by Burdette's men, Chance finds himself in a sticky situation. Bottom: Chance, Colorado, and Stumpy take up arms as they leave on a mission to rescue Dude.

THE HORSE SOLDIERS (1959)

UNITED ARTISTS

DIRECTOR: JOHN FORD

SCREENPLAY: JOHN LEE MAHIN AND MARTIN RACKIN

BASED ON THE NOVEL BY HAROLD SINCLAIR

PRINCIPAL CAST: JOHN WAYNE (COLONEL JOHN MARLOWE), WILLIAM HOLDEN (MAJOR HENRY "HANK" KENDALL), CONSTANCE TOWERS (HANNAH HUNTER), ALTHEA GIBSON (LUKEY), HOOT GIBSON (SERGEANT BROWN), JUDSON PRATT (SERGEANT MAJOR KIRBY), KEN CURTIS (CORPORAL WILKIE) AND WILLIS BOUCHEY (COLONEL SECORD)

The Horse Soldiers, John Ford's only full-length Civil War film (he directed the "Civil War" segment of *How the West Was Won,* 1962), is based on a novel by Harold Sinclair about a critical, 17-day mission by three Union cavalry regiments. In the spring of 1863, the war was going badly for the North. A desperate General Grant sent the three regiments under the command of Colonel Benjamin Grierson some 300 miles into Confederate territory to destroy a railroad supply line and bridge near Newton Station and Vicksburg.

United Artists reportedly paid its two stars, Wayne and William Holden, the then-unprecedented amount of $775,000 each, plus one-fifth of the net. Shot mostly in Louisiana and Mississippi, *The Horse Soldiers* is unusual in that it lacks the celebratory feeling of military camaraderie and glory that normally infuses Ford's cavalry films; this film is about the darker side of war.

Wayne plays Colonel John Marlowe, who resents being told he has to take a doctor along on the mission.

Top: Wayne as Colonel John Marlowe. Bottom: Officers meet in the field. Ford studied the Civil War photos of Matthew Brady in order to accurately capture the look of such gatherings.

The tension between Marlowe and the doctor, Major Hank Kendall (Holden), provides nearly as much conflict as do the skirmishes and battles. We learn that Marlowe's bitterness against doctors stems from a botched operation on his wife.

On the other hand, Marlowe has more in common with the doctor than he cares to admit. For one, neither is career army. Prior to the war, Marlowe was a railroad engineer; thus, the whole idea of destroying rail lines gives him no pleasure. Neither he nor Kendall carry a sidearm, and when they engage the enemy at Newton Station, Marlowe tells the doctor, with some anguish, "I didn't want this." Later, when the South sends boys from a local military school to attack them, Marlowe withdraws his troops rather than have them shoot at "kids." And when Southern women hurl dirt at him and his men as they ride through town, he understands their fury and does nothing. There's even a scene where Marlowe cradles a dying soldier who tells him, "Just hold on to me, sir, and write my ma. I'll be in your debt forever."

In a subplot, Southern belle Hannah Hunter (Constance Towers) is caught listening in on Union plans, forcing Marlowe to bring her and her attendant (Althea Gibson) along with his troops, lest the women alert the Confederates. Hunter is drawn to Marlowe, who finds her attractive, too, especially when she rolls up her sleeves to help Kendall attend to some wounded men.

The battle, field hospital and town scenes are shot with impressive realism, and while Civil War buffs may point to a few historic inaccuracies, most of the cinematic elements look and feel right — especially Wayne's complex performance.

Top: "Yankee go home!" As the Union cavalry passes through town, women throw dirt — one of many scenes that prompted critics to praise the film's realism. Bottom: "Now, this is going to hurt a little." Kendall (William Holden) and Hannah (Constance Towers) tend to a wounded Marlowe.

PART 3

1960-1969

JOHN WAYNE: 1960-1969

After pouring his money and soul into the production of *The Alamo* (1960), John Wayne focused on positioning his film as an Academy Award contender for Best Picture, despite mixed reviews. In his zeal to promote the film, however, Wayne erred by going the hyperbolic route; he launched a campaign that essentially said it was moviegoers' patriotic duty to support *The Alamo* and its all-American values. His heavy-handed approach did little to persuade Academy voters of the film's worth; *The Alamo* received just one Academy Award, for Best Sound.

While *The Alamo* performed decently at the box office, Wayne nevertheless took a hit financially and began working at a furious pace to recover his losses. During post-production on *The Alamo*, Wayne filmed *North to Alaska* (1960). He later starred in *The Comancheros* (1961), *Hatari!* (1962), *The Man Who Shot Liberty Valance* (1962) and *Donavon's Reef* (1963), his last film for mentor John Ford.

WAYNE'S LEADING LADIES, 1960-1969

CAPUCINE
North to Alaska (1960)

Discovered by producer/agent Charles K. Feldman, the French fashion model made her American film debut in *Song Without End* (1960), the Franz Liszt biopic starring Dirk Bogarde. Although the film was savaged by critics, Capucine received a Golden Globe nomination for her performance and went on to star in *The Pink Panther* (1964), *What's New, Pussycat?* (1965) and *The Honey Pot* (1967).

KIM DARBY
True Grit (1969)

Landing the plum role of Mattie Ross in the hit film version of the Charles Portis novel was a coup for the 21-year-old Darby. She later reteamed with *True Grit* co-star Glen Campbell for a film based on another Portis novel, *Norwood* (1970), which fizzled at the box office. Since the 1970s, Darby has focused more on the small screen, guest starring on such television series as *Baretta*, *Murder, She Wrote* and *The X-Files*.

RITA HAYWORTH
Circus World (1964)

Hailed as "The Great American Love Goddess" by *Life* magazine writer Winthrop Stuart in 1941, Hayworth was the era's top sex symbol and the dream girl of World War II servicemen. A gifted dancer, she partnered beautifully with Fred Astaire in two films: *You'll Never Get Rich* (1941) and *You Were Never Lovelier* (1942). In 1946, she scorched the screen as the femme fatale heroine in the film noir classic *Gilda*, co-starring Glenn Ford.

In 1965, while undergoing a routine physical exam for *In Harm's Way,* Wayne, a heavy smoker, discovered he had "the big C": lung cancer. Enduring major surgery, Wayne initially went along with his publicist's advice to hide his diagnosis. Soon thereafter, he reversed course and gave a candid interview to the *Los Angeles Herald Examiner.* His frank discussion of the disease and his advice to others to get a check-up brought him national acclaim. Wanting to move on, he made his next film, *The Sons of Katie Elder* (1965), before he was fully recuperated.

In 1965, protests against the Vietnam War were heating up around the country. Wayne was confounded by what he saw as the lack of support for America and its soldiers. He voiced his views often and began to plan the production of a pro-war movie, *The Green Berets* (1968). In between making movies such as *Cast a Giant Shadow* (1966), *The War Wagon* (1967) and *El Dorado* (1967), Wayne commissioned a screenplay, secured assistance from the Department of Defense and visited Vietnam to see the situation firsthand. His goal was to make a film that demonstrated why the American mission to stop a Communist take over of South Vietnam was crucial.

VERA MILES
The Man Who Shot Liberty Valance (1962) and *Hellfighters* (1968)

Crowned Miss Kansas in 1948, Miles parlayed her beauty queen title into a successful film and television career. After playing a small but pivotal role in *The Searchers* (1956), Miles signed a five-year contract with Alfred Hitchcock, who cast her in *The Wrong Man* (1957) and *Psycho* (1960); she was also set to star in Hitchcock's *Vertigo* (1958), but the role ultimately went to Kim Novak. Although Miles never attained above-the-title stardom, she worked steadily until

PATRICIA NEAL
In Harm's Way (1965)

The husky-voiced Kentucky native came to Hollywood by way of Broadway, where she had won a Tony Award for her performance in the 1946 production of Lillian Hellman's *Another Part of the Forest.* After an attention-getting performance opposite Gary Cooper in *The Fountainhead* (1949), Neal starred in films ranging from *The Day the Earth Stood Still* (1951) to *A Face in the Crowd* (1957). She won the Best Actress Academy Award for *Hud* (1963).

MAUREEN O'HARA
McLintock! (1963)

Prior to reteaming with the Duke for the boisterous western comedy *McLintock!* (1963), O'Hara struck box office gold with the Walt Disney film *The Parent Trap* (1961), starring Hayley Mills. She also joined James Stewart in *Mr. Hobbs Takes a Vacation* (1962) and Henry Fonda in *Spencer's Mountain* (1963). A gifted singer, O'Hara briefly starred on Broadway in the 1960 musical *Christine* and released two albums: *Love Letters from Maureen O'Hara* and *Maureen O'Hara Sings Her Favorite Irish Songs.*

By the time *The Green Berets* was released in June of 1968, public sentiment toward the war had deeply soured. The film was greeted with hostile reviews and ethical questions about the relationship between Wayne and the Pentagon. The resulting uproar caused audiences to fill the theaters and make *The Green Berets* one of the top movies of 1968.

In the wake of *The Green Berets,* Wayne completed *Hellfighters* (1968) and then took on the iconic role of Rooster Cogburn in *True Grit* (1969). Critics who had recently lambasted Wayne for *The Green Berets* now found themselves praising him. While working on his next film, *The Undefeated* (1969), Wayne began to hear the Oscar buzz about his performance in *True Grit.*

"A little clique back in the East has taken great satisfaction in reviewing my politics instead of my picture."

— Wayne on the scathing reviews of *The Green Berets*

Opposite page: Wayne and Chill Wills in *McLintock!* (1963). Top: Duke as the eldest of *The Sons of Katie Elder* (1965). Bottom: Wayne and Kim Darby in *True Grit* (1969).

THE ALAMO (1960)

MGM

DIRECTOR: JOHN WAYNE

SCREENPLAY: JAMES EDWARD GRANT

PRINCIPAL CAST: JOHN WAYNE (COLONEL DAVY CROCKETT), RICHARD WIDMARK (JIM BOWIE), LAURENCE HARVEY (COLONEL WILLIAM TRAVIS), LINDA CRISTAL (FLACA), RICHARD BOONE (GENERAL SAM HOUSTON), FRANKIE AVALON (SMITTY), CHILL WILLS (BEEKEEPER), KEN CURTIS (CAPTAIN ALMERON DICKINSON) AND PATRICK WAYNE (CAPTAIN JAMES BUTLER BONHAM)

The only film John Wayne ever directed solo, *The Alamo* was a passion project from beginning to end. Since the late 1940s, the star had dreamed of making his directorial debut with the story of the 1836 siege of the mission in San Antonio de Bexar, and had pitched it around Hollywood for years. Wayne intended to limit his screen presence to a cameo as General Sam Houston, but neither studio executives nor Texas investors would back a John Wayne film without John Wayne in a lead role. John Ford counseled Duke that he'd be taking on too much by producing, directing and acting, but Wayne had little choice but to don Davy Crockett's coonskin cap. Even with that concession, he had to put up a chunk of the film's then-astronomical $12 million budget himself.

The widescreen epic would have been easier to finance if Clark Gable and Burt Lancaster, Wayne's first choices for straight-backed Colonel William Travis and rowdy Jim Bowie respectively, hadn't turned down

Top: Davy Crockett (Wayne) meets Colonel William Travis (Laurence Harvey) while the young Smitty (Frankie Avalon) looks on. Bottom: The flamboyant Davy Crockett flirts with the Mexican beauty Flaca (Linda Cristal).

Top: Jim Bowie (Richard Widmark) and Davy Crockett listen defiantly to the terms offered by General Santa Ana's emissary. Bottom: Bowie, Crockett and their outnumbered cohorts fight off the Mexican Army.

the novice director. Similarly, the picture would have been cheaper to make had Wayne shot in Panama or Mexico, as he originally planned. He ultimately agreed to build the replica Alamo from the original blueprints outside Brackettville, Texas, a nearly two-year process. The 70mm production required some 1,600 horses and riders, a daunting but colorful array of Mexican Army costumes and 87 intense days. But fidelity to accuracy was far from Wayne's biggest challenge.

Just 10 days after production began, Ford showed up unannounced on the set. He parked himself next to the camera, watched Wayne shoot a take and barked, "Goddammit, Duke, that's no way to play it. Here, try it this way." After a few days of Ford undermining his authority, Wayne was desperate for a solution that wouldn't offend his mentor and old friend. Cinematographer William Clothier had the idea of giving Ford a camera and operator and dispatching him to shoot action sequences without the lead actors. All told, Ford spent 47 days on location over four visits, and his unit spent some $250,000 of Wayne's money. Both men maintained that none of the veteran director's footage made it into the final film, a tale that's since been disproved by film historians.

The Alamo ran nearly three and a quarter hours at its San Antonio premiere, and Wayne agreed to trim a half hour for the theatrical release. A genuine event nonetheless, Wayne's stirring salute to American patriotism, gallantry and sacrifice did better overseas than stateside (despite being banned in Mexico). The film garnered seven Academy Award nominations, including Best Picture, Best Supporting Actor (Chill Wills) and Best Song ("The Green Leaves of Summer," which cracked the Top 40), but only won Best Sound.

Although Wayne didn't recoup his investment in *The Alamo* until the network television rights were sold in 1971, he always remained deeply proud of his passion project.

NORTH TO ALASKA (1960)

TWENTIETH CENTURY FOX

DIRECTOR: HENRY HATHAWAY

SCREENPLAY: JOHN LEE MAHIN, MARTIN RACKIN AND CLAUDE BINYON

PRINCIPAL CAST: JOHN WAYNE (SAM MCCORD), STEWART GRANGER (GEORGE PRATT), FABIAN (BILLY PRATT), CAPUCINE (MICHELLE "ANGEL" BONET), ERNIE KOVACS (FRANKIE CANON), MICKEY SHAUGHNESSY (PETER BOGGS), KARL SWENSON (LARS NORDQUIST) AND KATHLEEN FREEMAN (LENA NORDQUIST)

John Wayne's distinctive walk and talk made him a favorite target of comic impersonators, but the Duke himself rarely got the opportunity to cut up, making *North to Alaska* a welcome change of pace. The rollicking western farce set in 1900 Nome and Seattle gave Wayne a chance to poke fun at his heroic screen persona. The lightweight comedy struck a chord with audiences. Released two weeks after Wayne's directorial debut *The Alamo* (1960), *North to Alaska*'s success delivered the welcome news that Wayne's star shone as brightly as ever.

Prospectors Sam McCord (Wayne) and George Pratt (Stewart Granger) strike gold, but George suffers romantic misfortune when his fiancé marries another. Sam finds George a new bride in prostitute Angel (Capucine), but she falls for Sam. If romantic complications were not enough, Sam and George face the devious machinations of conman Frankie Canon (Ernie Kovacs), and other claim jumpers after their mine.

That *North to Alaska* turned out as well as it did was something of a miracle, given that when Wayne arrived at the film's Point Mugu, California, location, he discovered there

Top: Wayne as Sam McCord. Bottom: Sam McCord (Wayne) attends the loggers picnic and wins the treeclimbing contest.

was no script. The Writers Guild had gone on strike before it could be written. That fact had already driven original director Richard Fleischer off the movie. His replacement, Henry Hathaway, resorted to improvisation, but that slowed the work down, sending the production behind schedule.

Capucine's presence in the film also grated on cast and crew. Agent Charlie Feldman was the movie's uncredited producer and he was determined to make the French actress, his girlfriend, a star. "She was all wrong for the part," Wayne said. "[*North to Alaska*] was fun to make and to watch, but damn it — I hate to badmouth a lady — Capucine was not very good."

Johnny Horton's title tune came out two months before the movie and hit it big. A primed audience rushed out to see the movie. Critics liked it, too. The *Chicago Daily Tribune* called *North to Alaska* "slam-bang slapstick," while *Variety* raved, "The three brawls director Henry Hathaway has staged are classics of the cinematic art of make-believe pugilistics." "Pleasantly boisterous," deemed the *New York Times*.

"Straddling the muddy terrain without benefit of his customary six-gun, [Wayne] proves that he can carry his tongue in his cheek with the same impregnable aplomb," the *Times* added. Wayne had demonstrated comic flair before, most notably in *The Quiet Man* (1952), but *North to Alaska* offered the best evidence yet that the Duke was one fine comedian.

Top: In one of many mud fights, Sam gets to the mine just in time to stop claim jumpers, but then has to deal with a partner who thinks he failed him. Bottom: Sam and Angel (Capucine) share a laugh. The Duke was not a fan of the French actress.

THE MAN WHO SHOT LIBERTY VALANCE (1962)

PARAMOUNT PICTURES

DIRECTOR: JOHN FORD

SCREENPLAY: JAMES WARNER BELLAH AND WILLIS GOLDBECK

BASED ON THE SHORT STORY BY DOROTHY M. JOHNSON

PRINCIPAL CAST: JOHN WAYNE (TOM DONIPHON), JAMES STEWART (U.S. SENATOR RANSOM "RANCE" STODDARD), VERA MILES (HALLIE STODDARD), LEE MARVIN (LIBERTY VALANCE), EDMOND O'BRIEN (DUTTON PEABODY), ANDY DEVINE (MARSHAL LINK APPLEYARD) AND WOODY STRODE (POMPEY)

There is an elegiac tone that hovers over John Ford's *The Man Who Shot Liberty Valance* entirely in keeping with a story that totes up the cost of modernity as the Old West fades away to make room for the new. The film's mournful quality is not just a product of theme. The director's association with star John Wayne stretched back nearly 35 years, ever since he hired the USC football player as an extra and set gooseherder on *Mother Machree* (1928). *The Man Who Shot Liberty Valance* was not their final collaboration, but it is their last great movie together. It is impossible to imagine the film without Wayne; the star's larger-than-life image as a man whose stoic bravery sets him apart from his peers is a key element of *The Man Who Shot Liberty Valance*.

When the film begins, Tom Doniphon (Wayne) is already dead. He was an old man, as are the friends who come back home to the small Western town of Shinbone to mourn him, U.S. Senator Ransom Stoddard (James

Top: Tom Doniphon (Wayne) strikes a typically watchful pose. Bottom: Senator Ransom "Rance" Stoddard (James Stewart) and wife Hallie (Vera Miles) arrive for a sad homecoming.

Stewart) and his wife, Hallie (Vera Miles). Stoddard is a local hero, the man who stood up to the outlaw Liberty Valance (Lee Marvin), an action that helped pave the way for a territory to become a state and launched Stoddard's political career. Stoddard remembers it differently, as he spins a tale emphasizing Doniphon's courage and his own naiveté as a "tenderfoot" Easterner in over his head in the Old West. But the men who hear Stoddard's tale have no interest in the truth; as local newspaper editor Maxwell Scott observes, "This is the West, sir. When the legend becomes fact, print the legend."

For two stars so closely associated with the western, *The Man Who Shot Liberty Valance* marked the first time that Wayne and Stewart worked together. It is the film that launched a thousand impressions, as Doniphon's snide nickname for Stoddard, "pilgrim," captured the imagination of comedians everywhere. Writing in his book *"Have You Seen …?,"* critic David Thomson complains about the casting of "elderly stars" playing younger men in Stoddard's extended flashback, noting that Stewart was 54 playing a man in his 20s in those scenes. "It is altogether regrettable, for the law student who is not a man of action does not need to be middle-aged, too," he writes.

What Thomson fails to take into account is that Ford was not casting actors in Wayne and Stewart, but the personas they brought with them from so many other films. Doniphon could be an older, sadder version

Top: "Stand and deliver!" Liberty Valance (Lee Marvin) robs the stage. Bottom: Pompey (Woody Strode), Tom, and Hallie tend to a wounded Rance.

of the Ringo Kid from *Stagecoach* (1939) or a cousin to John T. Chance, the character Wayne played in Howard Hawks' *Rio Bravo* (1959), while Stoddard shares the idealism of Stewart's freshman senator in Frank Capra's *Mr. Smith Goes to Washington* (1939) and the pacifism of his lawman in *Destry Rides Again* (1939). On the surface, *The Man Who Shot Liberty Valance* is an archetypal western tale of good versus evil, but on a deeper level, the movie mourns the loss of the freedom and wildness the West represents. The casting of Wayne and Stewart — two icons who evoke Hollywood's fading golden era — emphasizes that grief in a way that would have been impossible with younger actors in those roles.

For Wayne, it was a difficult shoot. Ford could be cruel (James Cagney once used one word, *malice*, to describe him to filmmaker Peter Bogdanovich), and Wayne was a favored target. On the *Liberty Valance* shoot, Ford liked to bring up Stewart's World War II heroism, while chiding Wayne for not serving at all. A bigger challenge for Wayne was getting a handle on his character. He was grateful when Ford gave him a bit of business of kicking a steak out of another character's hand and when Stewart talked Ford into not cutting their final scene together. "The kicking the steak and the last scene gave me enough strength to carry [Doniphon] through the picture," Wayne insisted.

"Liberty Valance is the toughest man south of the Picketwire — next to me."

— Tom Doniphon (Wayne)

Tom confronts Liberty over a ruined steak. Opposite page: A humiliated Rance has an audience in Tom and newspaperman Dutton Peabody (Edmond O'Brien).

"In *Liberty Valance*, he's got the flamboyant heavy…he's got Eddie O'Brien [as drunken newspaperman Peabody] doing the intelligent humor, he's got two or three other guys doing the jokes and Andy [Devine as the cowardly marshal] and Jimmy kicking the horseshit and the girl [Vera Miles] playing, 'I can't be in love with Duke because the girl's in love with Jimmy,' so what the hell? Where do I go?" Wayne remembered.

Appropriately for a film about the closing of the Old West, Ford abandoned the wide-open spaces of his beloved Monument Valley for the backlot at Paramount Studios when he made *The Man Who Shot Liberty Valance*. In a contemporary review in the *Chicago Reader*, critic Dave Kehr praised that decision: "For some, the stylization is a crippling flaw, but I find it sublime: the film takes place, through elegant flashbacks, in a past that is remembered more than lived; essences are projected over particulars." In 1962, *Variety* was not so complimentary, "[Ford and the screenwriters] have taken a disarmingly simple and affecting premise, developed it with craft and skill to a natural point of conclusion, and then have proceeded to run it into the ground, destroying the simplicity and intimacy for which they have striven."

"Duke relied on Ford very much to direct him. I think Duke was enamored of what Jack, Coach, Pop, whatever it was they called him had done for his career. I think Ford was very responsible for Wayne's tremendous persona."

— *The Man Who Shot Liberty Valance* co-star Lee Marvin

Ford's final western was *Cheyenne Autumn* (1964), but Wayne continued to work in the genre for the rest of his life, winning his lone Academy Award for his self-parodying performance in 1969's *True Grit*. But he would never make another western with as much emotional resonance as *The Man Who Shot Liberty Valance*. Underappreciated at the time of its release, *Liberty Valance* is now recognized as one of Ford's greatest films — a classic of the western genre that the National Film Registry selected for preservation as a "culturally, historically or aesthetically significant film" in 2007.

Tom teaches a reluctant Rance how to shoot, but later sneers that Rance "couldn't shoot his hat off his own head."

Top: Liberty and henchmen Floyd (Strother Martin) and Reese (Lee Van Cleef) test the freedom of the press by attacking Peabody. Bottom: Only one man will be left standing when Rance and Liberty meet for the last time.

HOW THE WEST WAS WON (1962)

MGM/CINERAMA

DIRECTORS: JOHN FORD, HENRY HATHAWAY AND GEORGE MARSHALL

SCREENPLAY: JAMES R. WEBB

PRINCIPAL CAST: JOHN WAYNE (GENERAL WILLIAM TECUMSEH SHERMAN), CARROLL BAKER (EVE PRESCOTT RAWLINGS), LEE J. COBB (MARSHAL LOU RAMSEY), HENRY FONDA (JETHRO STUART), CAROLYN JONES (JULIE RAWLINGS), KARL MALDEN (ZEBULON PRESCOTT), HARRY MORGAN (GENERAL ULYSSES S. GRANT), GREGORY PECK (CLEVE VAN VALEN), GEORGE PEPPARD (ZEB RAWLINGS), ROBERT PRESTON (ROGER MORGAN), DEBBIE REYNOLDS (LILITH "LILI" PRESCOTT), JAMES STEWART (LINUS RAWLINGS), ELI WALLACH (CHARLIE GANT), RICHARD WIDMARK (MIKE KING) AND SPENCER TRACY (NARRATOR)

Of the five narrative segments comprising *How the West Was Won*, "The Civil War," starring John Wayne, is generally regarded as the most artful and compelling portion of this epic saga. Based on a series of *Life* magazine articles, this grandly entertaining film was a critical and commercial blockbuster for MGM, which partnered with Cinerama to make the second narrative feature ever filmed in the mega-screen Cinerama process.

A veritable galaxy of stars was recruited for the project, and three directors were hired so filming could be completed in a financially feasible time span (with a single director, it would have taken at least two years). Fortunately, the narrative structure was conducive to this multi director approach: five separate segments covering three generations of one pioneering family over the course of 50 years, from 1839 to 1889. Henry Hathaway directed the first, second and last portions: "The Rivers," "The

Top: General Ulysses S. Grant (Harry Morgan) and General William Tecumseh Sherman (Wayne) pay a visit to the Union field hospital at Shiloh. Bottom: General Sherman demands a lantern before sitting down to a serious discussion with General Grant.

Top: A craggy General Sherman works to restore General Grant's shattered confidence the night after the first bloody battle at Shiloh. Bottom: General Sherman and General Grant are startled by an explosive shot fired from the pistol of a thwarted assassin.

Plains," and "The Outlaws"; George Marshall directed the fourth, "The Railroad"; and the legendary John Ford, the third and finest segment, "The Civil War."

In approaching Wayne, Ford asked him to reprise a role he had played on a classic 1960 episode of the TV series *Wagon Train:* Union General William Tecumseh Sherman. The two-day shoot in Paducah, Kentucky, reunited Wayne with Ford, who was then nearly 70 years old and winding down; many say "The Civil War" was his last truly great piece of work. Bypassing the schmaltz present in other parts of *How the West Was Won,* Ford gives us just enough imagery — a bloody creek, a night shrouded in a haze of gun smoke — to elicit the sense of a day (April 6, 1862) immortalized by slaughter. Under Ford's direction, Wayne downplays Sherman's notorious brutality and instead gives us a man less than eager to see his superior officer, General Ulysses S. Grant (Harry Morgan), resign and leave command of the Union army to him. As Wayne portrays him, Sherman seems to sense that being number two suits him fine; that Grant will eventually give the order to lay waste to the South, and he'll get to carry it out.

Like the roles of many of his fellow stars in *How the West Was Won* (1962), Wayne's is essentially a cameo — so don't just watch it for the Duke, but for the spectacular scenes throughout this bona-fide epic: a deadly raft-ride through whitewater rapids; a wagon train under attack by hostile Indians; a heart-stopping buffalo stampede; and one of the greatest train robbery sequences ever filmed. Nominated for eight Academy Awards, including Best Picture, *How the West Was Won* won three: Best Screenplay, Best Sound and Best Editing; the latter was particularly well deserved, considering the editing challenges created by the Cinerama process: an 800-pound camera recording a panoramic vista in three 35 mm strips of film.

Cinerama itself was short-lived, but *How the West Was Won* successfully lured viewers away from their television sets with the promise of a new and exciting theatrical experience.

DONOVAN'S REEF (1963)

PARAMOUNT PICTURES

DIRECTOR: JOHN FORD

SCREENPLAY: JAMES EDWARD GRANT

PRINCIPAL CAST: JOHN WAYNE (MICHAEL "GUNS" DONOVAN), LEE MARVIN (THOMAS "BOATS" GILHOOLEY), JACK WARDEN (DR. WILLIAM DEDHAM), ELIZABETH ALLEN (AMELIA DEDHAM), CESAR ROMERO (MARQUIS ANDRE DE LAGE) AND DOROTHY LAMOUR (MISS LAFLEUR)

*D*onovan's Reef was the 14th and final film that John Wayne made with director John Ford, and while most critics agreed with the *Variety* reviewer who groused that "Ford aficionados will squirm" through this light hearted western transplanted to the South Seas, all conceded that Wayne fans would love the film. As the reviewer for the *New York Times* summarized, it's "sheer contrivance effected in hearty, fun-loving, truly infectious style." And the location filming in Kauai makes this escapist fare even more of an escape.

During World War II, three American sailors were separated from their destroyer and landed on the fictional island of Haleakoloha, where they were hidden by locals and waged a guerrilla war against superior Japanese forces. But all that's in the past. Now, one of the men, Michael "Guns" Donovan (Wayne), is proprietor of Donovan's Reef saloon on that very same island where his friend, Dr. Dedham (Jack Warden), built a hospital and serves as the only doctor. And the third? He's a Merchant-Marine sailor named Thomas "Boats" Gilhooley (Lee Marvin), who jumps ship to keep

Top: After the brawl. Bottom: "Guns" Donovan (Wayne) helps Doc Dedham's daughter Amelia (Elizabeth Allen) into a dugout.

his annual appointment to brawl with Donovan, the man with whom he shares a birthday. But it's another visitor to the island who stirs things up even more. Amelia Dedham (Elizabeth Allen), who runs a shipping company for a staid Boston family, arrives to prove that her father — whom she's never met — isn't living a moral life by Boston standards, so she can keep him from inheriting the company. With the Doc making his rounds to another part of the island, what else is there to do but conspire to pretend that his three children, Lelani, Sally, and Luki (Jacqueline Malouf, Cherylene Lee, Jeffrey Byron) are Donovan's?

It's a romantic comedy, really, with drinking, smoking, brawling, and a welcome to the island song that keeps replaying every time new visitors arrive. This road trip also has some familiar faces, like Dorothy Lamour as a saloon singer, Cesar Romero as the governor who schemes to court Ms. Dedham because of her millions, Marcel Dalio as the children's tutor and local priest, and character actor Mike Mazurki, who plays the only police presence on the island. Wayne is clearly in his element, as comfortable in shorts and navy cap as he is chaps and a Stetson.

According to Allen, the film's wild shenanigans weren't confined to Ford's "takes." She remembers at least one night when Marvin was so drunk he tore off his clothes and danced a naked hula on the bar of his hotel. It's no wonder he was hung over and that shooting often had to be rescheduled for later in the day. But even Marvin's magnetic presence is dwarfed by the Duke, who's the "big kahuna" in *Donovan's Reef*.

Top: Donovan and Lelani (Jacqueline Malouf) on the ski-boat. Bottom: The lush Hawaiian scenery give a South Seas backdrop to a screenplay that's essentially a brawling western in the *McLintock!* (1963) mode.

McLintock! (1963)

United Artists

Director: Andrew V. McLaglen

Screenplay: James Edward Grant

Principal Cast: John Wayne (G.W. McLintock), Maureen O'Hara (Katherine McLintock), Patrick Wayne (Dev Warren), Stefanie Powers (Becky McLintock), Jack Kruschen (Jake Birnbaum), Chill Wills (Drago), Yvonne De Carlo (Mrs. Warren) and Jerry Van Dyke (Matt Douglas Jr.)

McLintock! is the closest John Wayne came to playing Shakespeare. His favorite screenwriter, James Edward Grant, based the original script on *The Taming of the Shrew*, and movie posters even depicted Wayne with co-star Maureen O'Hara over his knee, giving her a spanking. After the rollicking success of *North to Alaska* (1960), Wayne was eager to do another comedic western, and as *Variety* noted, "The style of production is forked-tongue-in-cheek." But what appealed to him most was the chance to work with O'Hara again.

Wayne plays G.W. McLintock, a cattle baron so wealthy and influential that the town he founded bears his name. Set during the time of the vanishing West, *McLintock!* offers plenty of reminiscing about the "good old days" when the territory was rougher and life was harsher. The conflict of this western isn't settlers vs. the elements, Native Americans, and outlaws, or even farmers vs. cattlemen; it's sophisticated folk vs. old-timers who remember the rough-and-tumble days and are still a little rough around the edges. The story is set in motion by the return of McLintock's wife, Katherine (O'Hara), from the

Top: Wayne as G.W. McLintock. Bottom: Both Wayne and O'Hara shivered in the cold bentonite that was made to look like mud in this scene.

East, where she'd gone after abandoning her husband because of his "crude" ways. Also returning is daughter Becky (Stefanie Powers), who had been away at college, and Comanche chief Puma (Michael Pate), who arrives with the other old chiefs to challenge a government ruling that would move them to a reservation. As the town prepares for a July 4 celebration, the narrative threads come together, and McLintock's efforts to deal with his headstrong wife are mirrored by the attempts of hired hand Dev Warren (Patrick Wayne) to best his "sophisticated" rivals for Becky's hand.

McLintock! was a family affair, with Wayne's sons Michael and Patrick taking producing and co-starring roles, respectively; even daughter Aissa has a bit part in the film. Shot in Nogales and Old Tucson, the film brought together some of Hollywood's best-known character actors, including Edgar Buchanan and Wayne stock players like Chill Wills, Bruce Cabot, Jack Kruschen and Hank Worden. It also produced one of the most memorable John Wayne movie lines: "Pilgrim, you caused a lot of trouble this morning, might have got somebody killed. And somebody out to belt you in the mouth. But I won't. I won't . . . the *hell* I won't!" Delivering that punch, Wayne initiates the mud-pit brawl that became the star's favorite scene and the centerpiece of this slapstick western comedy.

Most reviewers loved *McLintock!*, which turned a nice profit for United Artists. It was Wayne at his swaggering best — off-camera, too, as when he called reluctant stuntmen "chicken s--ts" for not wanting to go down a 50-foot slide, and then showed them how it was down.

Top: McLintock advocates on behalf of the Comanche. Bottom: A tense moment between McLintock and his estranged wife, Katherine (Maureen O'Hara).

CIRCUS WORLD (1964)

PARAMOUNT PICTURES

DIRECTOR: HENRY HATHAWAY

SCREENPLAY: BEN HECHT, JULIAN ZIMET AND JAMES EDWARD GRANT

STORY: PHILIP YORDAN AND NICHOLAS RAY

PRINCIPAL CAST: JOHN WAYNE (MATT MASTERS), CLAUDIA CARDINALE (TONI ALFREDO), RITA HAYWORTH (LILI ALFREDO), LLOYD NOLAN (CAP CARSON), RICHARD CONTE (ALDO ALFREDO) AND JOHN SMITH (STEVE MCCABE)

Based on a story by Philip Yordan and Nicholas Ray, *Circus World* casts Wayne as Matt Masters, the owner of a circus troupe at the turn of the century. En route to Spain to begin a European tour, the circus suffers a devastating setback when its ship capsizes. With his teenaged ward Toni (Claudia Cardinale), Matt works to rebuild the circus — and find his long-lost love, Toni's mother, Lili (Rita Hayworth), who vanished years earlier, following the tragic death of her husband, a trapeze artist.

With *It's a Wonderful Life* (1946) auteur Frank Capra directing and John Wayne starring, *Circus World* might have been something special. "I was sure in that big chunk of solid man there was the depth and humanity of a Mr. Deeds, a Mr. Smith, or a John Doe," Capra noted in his memoirs. But the director left the picture before shooting a single frame, reportedly due to friction with screenwriter James Edward Grant. The three-time Academy Award–winning director

Top: Circus owner Matt Masters (Wayne) reflects a moment on painful memories from the past. Bottom: Raised by her guardian Matt Masters since childhood, Toni Alfredo (Claudia Cardinale), has become a beautiful young woman.

Top: Matt Masters shares a dance with Lili Alfredo (Rita Hayworth). Bottom: Matt Masters gives a rousing speech to his circus troupe after disaster strikes.

never made another film and *Circus World*'s fortunes changed dramatically.

The tensions between Capra and Grant began when Grant airily told the director, "All you gotta have in a John Wayne picture is a hoity-toity dame with big tits that the Duke can turn over his knee and spank, and a collection of jerks he can smash in the face every five minutes." Taken aback by Grant's crude, devil-may-care approach, Capra resolved to write his own version of the *Circus World* screenplay. But when Wayne sided with Grant, Capra returned his $50,000 advance and handed the directorial reins to Henry Hathaway.

Capra's departure was only the beginning of the film's troubles, which reached their nadir on the day Hathaway filmed a circus fire tent sequence. Wayne barely escaped death when he missed his cue to vacate the burning set, only fleeing when he smelled his toupee burning and could no longer breathe.

Reviews were mixed and *Circus World* barely earned back its cost, despite a Golden Globe win for Best Song and a Best Actress nomination for Hayworth. Remarking that *Circus World* bore no comparison to Cecil B. DeMille's *The Greatest Show on Earth* (1952), the *New York Times*' Bosley Crowther was brutal, suggesting, "This one might be labeled the worst." *Time* found the circus milieu fun, but carped that the widescreen Cinerama presentation "magnifies a meager tale beyond all reasonable proportions."

Seen today, *Circus World* is enjoyable and colorful entertainment. Wayne conveys gravity, humor, and confidence. Ironically, perhaps smarting from his near-miss with Capra, the star turned out to be the movie's harshest critic. "I did the worst circus film ever made, and thinking back, I have to concede that my life was like a f---ing circus," Wayne said. "But I'll tell you something. I wouldn't have it any other way."

IN HARM'S WAY (1965)

PARAMOUNT PICTURES

DIRECTOR: OTTO PREMINGER

SCREENPLAY: WENDELL MAYES

BASED ON THE NOVEL BY JAMES BASSETT

PRINCIPAL CAST: JOHN WAYNE (REAR ADMIRAL ROCK TORREY), KIRK DOUGLAS (COMMANDER PAUL EDDINGTON JR.), PATRICIA NEAL (MAGGIE HAYNES), HENRY FONDA (ADMIRAL CHESTER NIMITZ) BURGESS MEREDITH (COMMANDER EGAN T. POWELL), BRANDON DE WILDE (ENSIGN JEREMIAH TORREY), DANA ANDREWS (VICE ADMIRAL B.T. "BLACKJACK" BRODERICK), PATRICK O'NEAL (COMMANDER NEAL OWYNN), TOM TRYON (LIEUTENANT WILLIAM "MAC" MCCONNELL), PAULA PRENTISS (BEVERLY MCCONNELL) AND STANLEY HOLLOWAY (CLAYTON CANFIL)

As melodramas go, few are as chock-full of incident as Otto Preminger's star-studded, gorgeous, black-and-white epic *In Harm's Way*. Alcoholism, adultery, rape, suicide and familial estrangements are elements in an otherwise straight World War II drama. Based on James Bassett's best-selling 1962 potboiler *Harm's Way*, the story of one naval officer's action-packed adventures offered John Wayne one more opportunity to shine as a silver screen war hero.

As the Japanese attack Pearl Harbor, Captain Rock Torrey (Wayne) and his men fight back. His reward is a demotion to desk duty, until the navy realizes he belongs in battle and promotes him to rear admiral. Torrey finds time for romance with nurse Maggie Haynes (Patricia Neal) and an uneasy reunion with his estranged son, Jeremiah (Brandon De Wilde), an ensign.

Top: Commander Paul Eddington Jr. (Kirk Douglas), civilian scout Clayton Canfil (Stanley Holloway), Rear Admiral Rockwell Torrey (Wayne), and Commander Egan Powell (Burgess Meredith) consider a plan of attack against the Japanese. Bottom: Lieutenant Maggie Haynes (Patricia Neal) and Rock Torrey share a moment of grief over a fallen friend.

Living up to his reputation as a bully, Preminger fired one actor, Chill Wills, for objecting to his browbeating, and he was particularly cruel to *In Harm's Way* co-star Tom Tryon, who had previously suffered Preminger's wrath while filming *The Cardinal* (1963). As Kirk Douglas remembered it, "He [Preminger] would come right up to Tom and scream until he was spitting saliva."

Preminger never yelled at Wayne, despite the fact the Duke had a persistent cough that sometimes ruined takes. The star would be diagnosed with lung cancer after the production wrapped, and his daughter Aissa remembered, "Even in the crystalline air of Hawaii, it became so torturous that some days he had to stop shooting his scenes."

Despite differences in politics and temperament, the two men mostly got along. Their one area of vehement disagreement was over Preminger's reliance on miniatures to supplement battle scenes. Wayne thought they destroyed the film's realism, but he couldn't persuade Preminger. "There was no way to tell him," Wayne said. "Goddamn, he wanted to have his picture taken on those miniatures."

The *New York Times'* Bosley Crowther dismissed *In Harm's Way* as "slick and shallow," but not all of the reviews were dismal. *Variety* raved, "The sea battle sequences are filmmaking at its best," while the *Hollywood Reporter* observed, "John Wayne is the best he has ever been in his career." Good notices failed to convince the public. *In Harm's Way* flopped at the box office, earning only $3.85 million, leaving the $5.43 million production in the red. It was a disappointment that brought Wayne's long World War II career to a quiet close.

Top: Rock Torrey and his long-estranged son Jeremiah (Brandon De Wilde) make peace with one another before war separates them again. Bottom: One of the spectacular battle scenes in *In Harm's Way*.

THE SONS OF KATIE ELDER (1965)

PARAMOUNT PICTURES

DIRECTOR: HENRY HATHAWAY

SCREENPLAY: WILLIAM H. WRIGHT, ALLAN WEISS AND HARRY ESSEX

STORY: TALBOT JENNINGS

PRINCIPAL CAST: JOHN WAYNE (JOHN ELDER), DEAN MARTIN (TOM ELDER), MARTHA HYER (MARY GORDON), MICHAEL ANDERSON JR. (BUD ELDER), EARL HOLLIMAN (MATT ELDER), JEREMY SLATE (BEN LATTA), JAMES GREGORY (MORGAN HASTINGS), PAUL FIX (SHERIFF BILLY WATSON), GEORGE KENNEDY (CURLEY) AND DENNIS HOPPER (DAVE HASTINGS)

A powerful undercurrent elevates *The Sons of Katie Elder* above the run-of-the-mill western, with that same subtext powerfully enhancing Wayne's lead performance. The theme here is not running away from one's obligations, a motif expressed in the isolation and responsibility that falls upon the shoulders of the oldest Elder brother, the one charged with setting things right for his family.

In this tale *very* loosely based on a true story, John Elder (Wayne) has joined his brothers Tom (Dean Martin), Matt (Earl Holliman) and Bud (Michael Anderson Jr.) as they bury their mother in a dusty Texas town where (with the exception of Bud, the youngest) they had virtually abandoned her. The Elder boys, now grown men with troubles of their own, feel less than welcome in Clearwater, and soon learn that their father, Bass Elder, was murdered some years back on the same day he lost the family ranch to gunsmith Morgan Hastings (James Gregory) in a game of blackjack. When it becomes apparent that Hastings' good fortune was more

Top: The Elder brothers (John Wayne, Dean Martin, Earl Holliman and Michael Anderson Jr.) strike a *Bonanza*-esque pose as they ride out to the ranch that their Pa supposedly gambled away. Bottom: John Elder (Wayne), his eyes betraying the isolation of the hardcore tough guy, glances back into the Clearwater Saloon after the sheriff breaks up a near gunfight.

Top: John Elder and his brother Matt (Earl Holliman), shackled together and caught in a potentially deadly ambush, attempt to escape by leaping into the river below. Bottom: John Elder, with his wounded brother Matt at his side and a six-shooter in each hand, fires back at his attackers from beneath a dynamited bridge.

than just a stroke of luck, the Elders must choose between leaving things as they stand and seeking out the truth. Goaded by John, a roughhewn gunslinger, the brothers choose truth and suffer the consequences, including the movie's set piece, a deadly ambush on a wooden bridge.

What heightens Wayne's performance here — in a part the *New York Times* said "fit him with bullet precision" — is the fact that, in real life, too, the actor had been making hard choices. In 1964, Wayne was diagnosed with cancer and underwent surgery to remove a lung tumor and two left ribs. In a drugged state following the operation, he'd taken the counsel of advisors and had lied about his condition, attributing his hospitalization to an abscess. Months later, in an exclusive interview with a columnist for the *Los Angeles Herald Examiner,* Wayne set the record straight: "I had the Big C, but I've beaten the son of a bitch."

He also chose to get back to work. "On January 4, I'll go to Durango, Mexico, to start *The Sons of Katie Elder.* It's a typical John Wayne western, so you know I have to be in good health. I didn't get famous doing drawing room comedies."

Not only did Wayne have to get back in front of a lens, he needed to do it as if nothing had changed. He had to be John Wayne, tough guy, again; his career depended on it. That meant he had to perform many of his own stunts, as no-nonsense director Henry Hathaway insisted, including jumping from the wagon on the bridge into the icy river below. The Duke came through his trial with good humor and his reputation intact.

To watch Wayne in *Katie Elder* is to see a 58-year-old man, packing too many pounds and less than comfortable in his ailing body, attempt to stay true to his man's man image: the guy who never lets his guard down and never lets fear take the reins. Wayne is appropriately heroic as John Elder, but there are moments when he reveals the fear lurking beneath his character's stoic façade. These moments give Wayne's performance a gravitas in a film that won the 1966 Western Heritage Award.

THE GREEN BERETS (1968)

WARNER BROS./SEVEN ARTS

DIRECTORS: RAY KELLOGG AND JOHN WAYNE

SCREENPLAY: JAMES LEE BARRETT

BASED ON THE NOVEL BY ROBIN MOORE

PRINCIPAL CAST: JOHN WAYNE (COLONEL MIKE KIRBY), DAVID JANSSEN (GEORGE BECKWORTH), JIM HUTTON (SERGEANT PETERSEN), ALDO RAY (MASTER SERGEANT MULDOON), RAYMOND ST. JACQUES (SERGEANT DOC MCGEE), BRUCE CABOT (COLONEL MORGAN), JACK SOO (COLONEL CAI), GEORGE TAKEI (CAPTAIN NIM), PATRICK WAYNE (LIEUTENANT JAMISON), LUKE ASKEW (SERGEANT PROVO) AND IRENE TSU (LIN)

It was 1968, and the Vietnam War was tearing America apart. *The Green Berets*, starring and co-directed by John Wayne, was just one more shot of gasoline tossed on the flames. Delve into accounts of the film's debut and you're sure to find the opening salvo of Renata Adler's 1968 review for *The New York Times*: "The Green Berets is a film so unspeakable, so stupid, so rotten and false in every detail…" South Carolina's Strom Thurmond responded on the Senate floor, citing the *Times'* praise for the musical *Hair* as further evidence of its contempt for everything "patriotic and pro-America."

Certainly *The Green Berets*, Hollywood's most ambitious film about the Vietnam War produced *during* the Vietnam War, is pure propaganda — i.e., war brings out the best in us and the worst in them. Though Wayne always claimed that he was given no free ride from the government — *The Green Berets* was filmed at Fort Benning, Georgia, with Uncle Sam providing the hardware — his character, Colonel Mike Kirby, often comes across as a mouthpiece for the Pentagon.

Top: Colonel Mike Kirby (Wayne) and his military driver in Da Nang. Bottom: Kirby and his men advance during a nighttime firefight with the Vietcong.

When Columbia Pictures, which owned the rights to Robin Moore's best-selling novel *The Green Berets,* couldn't come up with a script acceptable to the military, the studio sold the rights to Wayne for $50,000. He pulled strings at Warner Bros. and was soon teaming with Ray Kellogg to direct a film he later claimed was more about supporting our boys than the war. Yet Wayne's pro-war stance pervades *The Green Berets*, particularly during the film's heavy-handed first hour.

Fortunately, *The Green Berets* shifts into action-film-mode in the film's second half. At the behest of Warner Bros., which wanted Wayne to make a war film, not a propaganda piece, character-enriching scenes with Kirby's wife (played by Vera Miles) were excised from the final print. Instead, most of the film's second hour depicts a fierce firefight, when the Vietcong overrun an encampment of South Vietnamese civilians protected by Kirby and his Special Forces. Despite some cheesy effects, improbable weaponry and decidedly non-Vietnamese extras, there's some genuine excitement in these scenes, even if accuracy is not the film's strong suit.

Still, for all its many flaws, *The Green Berets* overcame uniformly negative reviews to gross $11 million at the box office, an impressive number in 1968. Wayne had help with his directing — not from the credited Ray Kellogg, whom nobody remembers being on the set, but from veteran Mervyn LeRoy, whom Warner Bros. sent in at the eleventh hour to make sure things were on track. But as an actor, Wayne needed no help; it was his special gift that he could successfully pull off a character like Colonel Kirby in the midst of a clunky film and an impossible war.

Top: Kirby gives a sip of bourbon to the mortally wounded Sergeant Provo (Luke Askew). Bottom: Kirby places Sergeant Petersen's green beret on the head of South Vietnamese orphan Hamchunk (Craig Jue).

TRUE GRIT (1969)

PARAMOUNT PICTURES

DIRECTOR: HENRY HATHAWAY

SCREENPLAY: MARGUERITE ROBERTS

BASED ON THE NOVEL BY CHARLES PORTIS

PRINCIPAL CAST: JOHN WAYNE (MARSHAL REUBEN J. "ROOSTER" COGBURN),
KIM DARBY (MATTIE ROSS), GLEN CAMPBELL (LA BOEUF), ROBERT DUVALL
(NED PEPPER), DENNIS HOPPER (MOON), JEREMY SLATE (EMMETT QUINCY),
STROTHER MARTIN (COLONEL G. STONEHILL) AND JEFF COREY (TOM CHANEY)

In the fifth decade of his movie career, John Wayne won his first and only Academy Award for Best Actor. His layered performance in *True Grit* includes elements of many other great Wayne characters, but combines them in a way that was fascinating and new, and genuinely different from the roughly 160 characters he had previously brought to the screen. Wayne had been pleased with many of his films and performances over the years, and had watched awards go instead to faddish films and of-the-moment stars, so recognition for *True Grit* was surprising and sweet. He graciously accepted it as the nod of approval for a lifetime of work.

Wayne knew *True Grit* was something special when he read the book by Charles Portis, and he committed to making the film quickly after reading the screenplay by Marguerite Roberts, declaring it the best script he had ever read. His character was no saint — he was crude and drank too much — but Wayne saw the goodness

Top: Marshal "Rooster" Cogburn (Wayne) delivers a fresh load of prisoners to the courthouse. Bottom: La Boeuf (Glen Campbell) proudly shows off the turkey he shot to the unimpressed Rooster Cogburn and Mattie Ross (Kim Darby).

beneath his grizzled exterior and was proud to take on the role of Rooster Cogburn. Henry Hathaway, who had directed Wayne in a variety of films over a 30-year period, was enlisted as director. Filming took place in small towns and the countryside near Aspen, Colorado, in the autumn of 1968.

True Grit begins with the cold-blooded murder of an innocent man by the outlaw Tom Chaney (Jeff Corey). Mattie Ross (Kim Darby), the victim's teenage daughter, vows that she'll personally track down the killer and see him hanged. To help in her quest for vengeance, she seeks out the toughest marshal she can find — a man with "true grit," she says — and hires Marshal Reuben J. "Rooster" Cogburn (Wayne), a leathery lawman who resides in the back of a Chinese grocery with a jug of liquor and a cat.

Before the unlikely duo can set out, they meet a Texas Ranger named La Boeuf (Glen Campbell) who is after Chaney for a different murder, and the three agree to join forces for the hunt. They head into the mountains where they know Chaney has joined a band of outlaws led by Cogburn's nemesis, Ned Pepper (Robert Duvall). Remarking that "She reminds me of me," Cogburn develops a paternal approach toward Mattie, calling her "baby sister" and deriding La Boeuf for lacking the toughness of his teenage patron. But when they finally catch up with Chaney, the three work together loyally, even risking their lives to save the others. The action

Top: Rooster Cogburn captures two members of the outlaw gang, played by Jeremy Slate and Dennis Hopper. Bottom: Mattie Ross lets Rooster Cogburn know that she intends to stay with him every step of the way.

scenes are thrilling throughout *True Grit*, and the final confrontation, with Cogburn charging Pepper and his gang, reins in his teeth and guns blazing, is one of the greatest showdowns in motion picture history.

Kim Darby's portrayal as the tenacious tomboy Mattie Ross provides the perfect contrast to Wayne's hardened Rooster Cogburn, but during filming Wayne complained that he was baffled by her acting style. Several prominent actresses, including Mia Farrow, Sondra Locke and Tuesday Weld, had been approached to play Mattie and turned the role down. Although she was a virtual unknown at the time, the 21-year-old Darby had appeared on several television series and could convincingly play a teenager. Wayne later admitted that his extended scene with Darby, in which Cogburn recounts his personal history to Mattie, was probably the best scene he ever did in his career.

Casting for the part of La Boeuf, the producers wanted a name to draw young moviegoers. Elvis Presley was approached about the role, but his manager insisted on Presley receiving top billing, above Wayne. Singer Glen Campbell was finally deemed to be the best fit, even though he had virtually no acting experience. However, he was enormously popular at the time, so the singer snared the meaty

"You're no bigger than a corn nubbin. What're you doing with all this pistol?"

— Rooster Cogburn (Wayne) to Mattie Ross (Kim Darby)

Rooster Cogburn tells Mattie Ross about the wife and son he left behind.

role opposite Wayne. In addition to playing La Bouef, Campbell recorded the *True Grit* theme song.

Rooster Cogburn and Mattie Ross spy the Pepper gang and plan their next move.

The production of *True Grit* was marred by frequent clashes between Wayne and two cast members, Dennis Hopper and Robert Duvall. Hopper reportedly angered Wayne to the point of violence. As for Duvall, he incurred the wrath of Wayne by challenging the director's choices one too many times. Less contentious were the excellent supporting players Jeremy Slate as Emmett Quincy, a member of Pepper's gang, and Strother Martin as the surly horse trader Colonel G. Stonehill.

True Grit opened in July 1969 at New York City's Radio City Music Hall, and critics were quick to herald it as masterful achievement. The day after its premiere, Vincent Canby predicted in his *New York Times* review that it would stand as one of the year's best films, calling it "a marvelously rambling frontier fable packed with extraordinary incidents, amazing encounters, noble characters and virtuous rewards.... The last scene in the movie is so fine it will probably become Wayne's cinematic epitaph."

On April 7, 1970, when Wayne took the stage at the Dorothy Chandler

"Baby sister, I was born game and I intend to go out that way."

— Rooster Cogburn (Wayne) to Mattie Ross (Kim Darby)

Ned Pepper (Robert Duvall) warns his pursuers to keep their distance.

Pavilion in Los Angeles to accept the Academy Award for Best Actor, he was visibly moved and told the audience, "If I'd known what I know now, I'd have put a patch on my eye 35 years ago." The crowd rose to its feet, showering him with the affection of an industry toward one of its most important figures: a veteran who had worked his way up from props and stunt jobs to become the biggest movie star in the world.

As if to demonstrate the hard work that got him there, Wayne returned to work the next day, flying down to Old Tucson, Arizona to continue filming *Rio Lobo* (1970) with director Howard Hawks. When he arrived on the set, the entire cast and crew greeted him wearing black eye patches. Wayne was moved to happy tears.

"Well, come see a fat old man sometime!"

— Rooster Cogburn (Wayne) to Mattie Ross (Kim Darby)

"Fill your hand, you son of a bitch!"

— Rooster Cogburn (Wayne) to Ned Pepper (Robert Duvall)

Top: Rooster Cogburn chides La Boeuf for letting Ned Pepper escape. Bottom: A drunken Rooster Cogburn tells his partners how he plans to catch the Pepper gang.

THE UNDEFEATED (1969)

TWENTIETH CENTURY FOX

DIRECTOR: ANDREW V. MCLAGLEN

SCREENPLAY: JAMES LEE BARRETT

STORY: STANLEY HOUGH

PRINCIPAL CAST: JOHN WAYNE (COLONEL JOHN HENRY THOMAS), ROCK HUDSON (COLONEL JAMES LANGDON), ANTONIO AGUILAR (GENERAL ROJAS), ROMAN GABRIEL (BLUE BOY), MARIAN MCCARGO (ANN LANGDON), LEE MERIWETHER (MARGARET LANGDON), MERLIN OLSEN (LITTLE GEORGE), MELISSA NEWMAN (CHARLOTTE LANGDON), BRUCE CABOT (JEFF NEWBY), JAN MICHAEL VINCENT (BUBBA WILKES), BEN JOHNSON (SHORT GRUB), EDWARD FAULKNER (ANDERSON), HARRY CAREY JR. (WEBSTER), PAUL FIX (GENERAL JOE MASTERS) AND ROYAL DANO (MAJOR SANDERS)

Rock Hudson wasn't being entirely fair when he summed up *The Undefeated* as "crap." Yes, the score is annoyingly obtrusive, the ending anticlimactic, and, as Confederate Colonel James Langdon, Hudson did have to wear a ridiculous feathered cap. That said, *The Undefeated* features Wayne tossing off some classic zingers, several impressive action sequences and an intriguing story line, set against the backdrop of the French attempt to regain a stronghold in North America by helping themselves to Mexico.

In his third film with director Andrew V. McLaglen, Wayne portrays Union Colonel John Henry Thomas. In the aftermath of the Civil War, Thomas has resigned his military commission so he can make a little money driving thousands of horses up from Mexico to sell to the U.S. Army. Divorced and sick of bloodshed, Thomas would rather be driving the horses south the border in lawless

Top: Colonel John Henry Thomas (Wayne) and Colonel James Langdon (Rock Hudson) put their differences aside over a bottle of bourbon. Bottom: Showing his softer side, Colonel Thomas tells Colonel Langdon's widowed sister Ann (McCargo) why his marriage went sour.

Top: Thomas and Langdon recover from blows they received during the big brawl at the Confederate camp in Mexico. Bottom: Thomas and Langdon lead thousands of horses toward the Mexican village where the Juaristas are holding the Confederates hostage.

Mexico than back in "civilization." But Thomas can't entirely escape his past when he's thrown together with Confederate Colonel James Langdon (Hudson), who's leading a party of settlers in pursuit of a fresh start in Mexico. Facing attacks by bandits and revolutionaries, the former adversaries reluctantly join forces to lead their respective parties to safety.

Taking a role originally intended for James Arness, Hudson established an immediate rapport with Wayne; the two regularly played chess on the set. Although Hudson's homosexuality was an "open secret" in Hollywood circles, it was apparently a non-issue for Wayne, as he later told a journalist in an interview quoted in Michael Munn's *John Wayne: The Man Behind the Myth*:

> Who the hell cares if he's a queer? ... I admit, I couldn't understand how a guy with those looks and that build and the ... *manly* ways he had about him could have been a homosexual, but it never bothered me. Life's too short.

Fresh from scoring his biggest hit in years with *True Grit* (1969), Wayne delivers a bravura performance in *The Undefeated* opposite Hudson, who seems a bit cowed by his larger-than-life co-star. The supporting cast is headed by NFL great Roman Gabriel, making his feature film debut as Blue Boy, Thomas' adopted Native American son. Several former Wayne co-stars and longtime cronies also play roles in *The Undefeated*, including Bruce Cabot, Ben Johnson and Harry Carey Jr.

Released in November 1969 to middling reviews, *The Undefeated* nevertheless did solid business at the box office. Thirty years after he achieved stardom in *Stagecoach*, the 62-year-old Wayne was at the very top of his game.

PART 4

1970-1976

OHN WAYNE: 1970-1976

s 1970 drew to a close, John Wayne sat down for an interview with *Playboy* magazine writer Richard Warren Lewis. Sensing that Wayne might have an interesting take on the shifting trends in the cultural landscape, Lewis peppered the star with questions on a e of hot-button issues. When the interview appeared in *Playboy*'s May 1971 issue, it featured w of controversial quotes from Wayne, who sounded off on everything from the history ative Americans to the civil rights movement. Non- apologetic, strident and decisively arch-ervative, John Wayne's opinions hit the pages and made the issue one of *Playboy*'s bestsellers.

Although Wayne remained a top-10 box office draw in the early 1970s, he enjoyed only ty success after *True Grit* (1969). He turned down the title role in *Dirty Harry* (1971) decision he came to regret when the film became a smash hit for Clint Eastwood. In onse, Wayne made two urban crime dramas in the *Dirty Harry* mold, *McQ* (1974) and nigan (1975), but neither film fared well with critics or audiences.

WAYNE'S LEADING LADIES, 1970-1976

MARGRET
in Robbers (1973)

punching bag in the 1960s — the er's Pauline Kael nastily called wd mechanical doll" — Ann-Mar- nced her detractors by giving an v Award–nominated performance ichols' *Carnal Knowledge* (1971). iter, she suffered devastating in- er falling 22 feet from a Lake Ta- e, but Ann-Margret resumed per- after a 10-week convalescence. she received a second Academy

LAUREN BACALL
The Shootist (1976)

Twenty-one years after *Blood Alley* (1955), Bacall reunited with Wayne to co-star in his final film. She would go on to win her second Tony Award for the musical *Woman of the Year* in 1981 and receive a Best Sup-porting Actress nomination for *The Mirror Has Two Faces* (1996). A 1997 Kennedy Center Honoree, Bacall subsequently won acclaim for her performances in two films with Nicole Kidman, *Dogville* (2003) and *Birth* (2004).

COLLEEN DEWHURST
The Cowboys (1972)

A powerful presence even in minor roles, Dewhurst played mostly supporting roles in such films as *A Fine Madness* (1966), the Duke's *McQ* (1974) and *When a Strang-er Calls* (1979). On Broadway, however, the Canadian-born character actress was a major star, renowned for her performanc-es in the plays of Eugene O'Neill. She won a Tony Award for the 1974 revival of the playwright's *A Moon for the Misbegotten*. Dewhurst also won four Emmy Awards for

While his film career seemed to be winding down, Wayne didn't lack for publicity. Never shy about voicing his opinions, he complained that the press was too hard on President Nixon during the Watergate scandal; Nixon had personally assured him that he had no role in the cover-up. Later, when the truth about Nixon's Watergate role was revealed, Wayne felt betrayed.

It was also during this time that Wayne's relationship with his third wife, Pilar, ended. Wayne did not want a divorce, fearing the effect it would have on their three children, but the two did separate. Shortly thereafter, Wayne began a relationship with his secretary, Pat Stacy, which lasted until the day he died.

In 1975, Wayne made the sequel to *True Grit* (1969), *Rooster Cogburn* (1975). Although he enjoyed working with Katharine Hepburn, he was burdened with a hacking cough that sometimes slowed production. His declining health also affected the production of what became his last film, *The Shootist* (1976).

KATHARINE HEPBURN
Rooster Cogburn (1975)

At an age when most of her screen contemporaries had either retired or were reduced to playing supporting roles, Hepburn continued to headline A-list film projects. Six years after her inspired teaming with Wayne in *Rooster Cogburn*, she won her fourth Best Actress Academy Award for *On Golden Pond* (1981), co-starring Henry Fonda. In 1999, the American Film Institute named Hepburn the greatest fe-

MAUREEN O'HARA
Big Jake (1971)

After marrying her third husband in 1968, O'Hara all but retired from acting; she nevertheless agreed to join the Duke for their fifth and final film together, *Big Jake* (1971). Twenty years would pass before O'Hara, now widowed, stepped before the cameras again to play an overbearing mother in the comedy *Only the Lonely* (1991). She published her autobiography, *'Tis Herself*, in 2004.

JENNIFER O'NEILL
Rio Lobo (1970)

A 1960s-era cover girl, O'Neill successfully made the leap from model to actress in the 1970s, starring in such films as *Summer of '42* (1971), *The Reincarnation of Peter Proud* (1975) and Luchino Visconti's last film, *The Innocent* (1976). In the 1980s, she starred in two short-lived television series, *Bare Essence* (1982) and *Cover Up* (1984). Now a born-again Christian, she heads the Jennifer O'Neill

In the following years, Wayne found himself in and out of hospitals with an array of various medical issues. Yet, he still managed to cause another political firestorm in 1977 when he publicly supported President Jimmy Carter's signing of the Panama Canal Treaty. A staunch Republican for years, Wayne was surprised by the fierce response he received from the right wing of his party and his friend, Ronald Reagan.

Because of his political views, Wayne was a polarizing figure in Hollywood. But when he walked onstage at the 1979 Academy Awards ceremony to present the Best Picture award to *The Deer Hunter* (1978), the audience greeted him with warm applause. He tried to appear healthy, even going so far as to wear a wet suit under his tuxedo to give the illusion of heft, but nothing could hide Wayne's gaunt figure. It was his last public appearance. On June 11, 1979, John Wayne succumbed to stomach cancer and died.

"I've played the kind of man I'd like to have been."

— Wayne

Wayne in his last film for director Howard Hawks: *Rio Lobo* (1970).

"My advice to any actor who wants to work in outdoor pictures is to learn to fight. Learn to hit and learn to roll with a punch. Learn to handle your body easily and smoothly. You have to make it look good. Above all, it has to be convincing."

— Wayne

Top: The Duke in the title role of *Big Jake* (1971). Bottom: Wayne reprised one of his most beloved roles in *Rooster Cogburn* (1975).

RIO LOBO (1970)

PARAMOUNT PICTURES

DIRECTOR: HOWARD HAWKS

SCREENPLAY: LEIGH BRACKETT AND BURTON WOHL

PRINCIPAL CAST: JOHN WAYNE (CORD MCNALLY), JORGE RIVERO (PIERRE CORDONA), JENNIFER O'NEILL (SHASTA DELANEY), JACK ELAM (PHILLIPS), VICTOR FRENCH (KETCHAM), SUSANA DOSAMANTES (MARIA CARMEN), CHRIS MITCHUM (TUSCARORA PHILLIPS), MIKE HENRY (HENDRICKS) AND SHERRY LANSING (AMELITA)

Leave it to John Ford to put John Wayne in his place, as the filmmaker did while visiting the set of Howard Hawks' *Rio Lobo*. After Hawks decided to print a first take of a scene featuring Wayne, Ford called the star over and barked at him, "Just 'cause you've won that damn Oscar, you're no actor. It usually takes 18 takes to get a performance out of you." Wayne, who was 63 years old at the time and the nation's top box office draw, simply said, "Yes sir."

The star's age is touched on repeatedly throughout *Rio Lobo*, most humorously in a scene with Wayne's much younger leading lady, Jennifer O'Neill, who plays Shasta Delaney. Choosing to share the bedroll of Union Army Colonel Cord McNally (Wayne) rather than a younger man, she explains that Cord's "old" and "comfortable." Taken aback, McNally replies, "I've been called a lot of things, but *comfortable*?"

Set primarily in Civil War–era Texas, the entertaining but uneven *Rio Lobo* is chiefly remembered for two vivid

Top: "I'll buy you a drink, if you don't mind drinkin' with a blue belly." When *Rio Lobo* first played in theaters, audiences were surprised when a Civil War film abruptly turned into a western, with former enemies now friends. Bottom: Hawks had a little fun with Wayne's age in *Rio Lobo*, as in this scene with Jennifer O'Neill.

scenes: a beautiful woman Amelita (future Paramount Pictures chairman Sherry Lansing) gets revenge on the man who scarred her, and the film's lively opening sequence in which Confederate soldiers use a hornets' nest and ropes to rob a Yankee train of its gold, causing the death of McNally's best friend in the process. When the war ends, McNally buys a drink for Pierre Cardona (Jorge Rivero), the leader of those Confederates, and his sergeant, Tuscarora Phillips (Chris Mitchum), letting them know he has no hard feelings. They were just doing their duty. It's the traitors who sold them the information that McNally wants. So when Phillips sends word that one of the traitors, the albino Whitey Carter (Robert Donner), is in Rio Lobo, Texas, where he's trying to steal the ranch of Phillips' father, McNally and Rivero team up to give Rio Lobo's citizens back their town, which had been stolen by a man named Ketcham (Victor French). It is a familiar theme of Hawks' films — former adversaries put aside their differences to join forces against a common enemy.

Hawks said that Wayne ad-libbed a number of scenes, including one where he finds the man he's been searching for and just starts pummeling him. Wayne said he was following his instincts, and so Hawks shot it that way. Despite his age and diminished breathing from successful lung cancer surgery, Wayne is still imposing as ever in *Rio Lobo*. When the bad sheriff says, "I shoulda taken you this morning," Wayne's character responds, "You shoulda *tried.*"

An unofficial remake of Hawks' far superior *Rio Bravo* (1959), *Rio Lobo* was mostly panned by critics, who objected to the film's lack of narrative momentum and the mediocre performances by Wayne's co-stars. *Variety*'s critic complained that "it is the same plot that has been worked over since the silent days of Bronco Billy with no new surprises. … Hawks' direction is as listless as the plot."

Although *Rio Lobo* performed decently at the box office, Hawks never directed another film. Wayne, however, wasn't quite ready to ride off into the Hollywood sunset.

Top: Veteran character actor Jack Elam (center) is a no-nonsense complement to Wayne in *Rio Lobo*. Bottom: Still riding tall in the saddle: Wayne as McNally in Howard Hawks' last film, *Rio Lobo*.

BIG JAKE (1971)

NATIONAL GENERAL PICTURES

DIRECTOR: GEORGE SHERMAN

SCREENPLAY: HARRY JULIAN FINK AND R.M. FINK

PRINCIPAL CAST: JOHN WAYNE (JACOB MCCANDLES), RICHARD BOONE (JOHN FAIN), PATRICK WAYNE (JAMES MCCANDLES), CHRIS MITCHUM (MICHAEL MCCANDLES), BRUCE CABOT (SAM SHARPNOSE), MAUREEN O'HARA (MARTHA MCCANDLES), GLENN CORBETT (O'BRIEN), JOHN DOUCETTE (CAPTAIN BUCK DUGGAN) AND BOBBY VINTON (JEFF MCCANDLES)

Westerns underwent a transformation in the late 1960s and 1970s, as directors with a talent for the visceral, such as Sam Peckinpah and Sergio Leone, gained ascendance. The genre was becoming bloodier and more violent. John Wayne's westerns bucked this trend until *Big Jake*. While it lacks the grandiose bloodletting of films like *The Wild Bunch* (1969), its ferocious climax and Wayne's galvanizing performance proved that the 64-year-old star was still vital and more than capable of holding his own in contemporary fare.

Martha McCandles (Maureen O'Hara) reaches out to her estranged husband Jake (Wayne) after outlaw John Fain (Richard Boone) kidnaps their grandson, Little Jake (Ethan Wayne). Jake agrees to deliver the million-dollar ransom, but he has other ideas about the best way to free the boy, setting his plan in motion with the help of sons James (Patrick Wayne) and Michael (Christopher Mitchum), and his Apache friend, Sam (Bruce Cabot).

Big Jake was a real Wayne family affair, with sons Patrick and eight-year-old Ethan in the cast, and eldest

Top: Wayne's entrance as the title character in *Big Jake*.
Bottom: *Big Jake* demonstrated Wayne's staying power and continued appeal as an movie star.

child Michael producing. It was Wayne's fifth film with O'Hara, and his ninth with Harry Carey Jr. They had first worked together in *Red River* (1948), when Carey was 27 years old.

Big Jake is a modern western, but the mood behind the scenes was more nostalgic. Several longtime Wayne collaborators worked on the film, including cinematographer William H. Clothier, who had shot more than a dozen Wayne features, including *Fort Apache* (1948) and *The Alamo* (1960), and composer Elmer Bernstein, who had scored four previous Wayne films, beginning with *The Comancheros* (1961). Wayne went back even further with director George Sherman. *Big Jake* marked the first time in 32 years that the two had worked together, but in 1938 and 1939, Sherman directed Wayne in all eight of the actor's "Three Mesquiteers" two-reelers.

The movie's melding of old western hands to new Hollywood sensibilities charmed the critics. "*Big Jake* is an inescapably likable John Wayne western," wrote *Time*'s Jay Cocks. The climax was "a murderous pip," according to the *New York Times'* Howard Thompson, who added, "The shadowy stealth, a church tower, a killer Collie, a flashing machete and the spitting guns add up to a horrifying humdinger." Audiences were just as responsive. A box office success, *Big Jake* served to sustain the Duke's reputation while also appealing to a new, younger generation of moviegoers.

Top: *Big Jake* is the fifth and final film pairing Wayne with his all-time favorite leading lady, Maureen O'Hara. Bottom: Much of *Big Jake* was filmed in Durango, Mexico, where Wayne had shot several films.

THE COWBOYS (1972)

WARNER BROS. PICTURES

DIRECTOR: MARK RYDELL

SCREENPLAY: WILLIAM DALE JENNINGS, IRVING RAVETCH AND HARRIET FRANK JR.

BASED ON THE NOVEL BY JENNINGS

PRINCIPAL CAST: JOHN WAYNE (WIL ANDERSEN), ROSCOE LEE BROWNE (JEBEDIAH NIGHTLINGER), BRUCE DERN (ASA WATTS), COLLEEN DEWHURST (KATE), ROBERT CARRADINE (SLIM HONEYCUTT), A. MARTINEZ (CIMARRON) AND SLIM PICKENS (ANSE)

An offbeat western that blends a gentle coming-of-age drama with a violent tale of youthful revenge, *The Cowboys* is an uncommonly beautiful film, shot on location in New Mexico and Colorado by Academy Award–winning cinematographer Robert Surtees. Wayne heads a fine cast of veteran characters and acting novices in Mark Rydell's big-screen version of William Dale Jennings' novel.

In 1870s-era Montana, rancher Wil Andersen (Wayne) needs hands to help drive his cattle to market in South Dakota. Since all the able-bodied men are off chasing a gold rush, he turns to local schoolboys, the oldest of whom, Slim (Robert Carradine) and Cimarron (A. Martinez) are only 15 years old. Out on the trail, as Andersen molds the kids to his exacting expectations of what good cowboys ought to be, his charges begin to grow up under his stern tutelage. What begins as a child's dream of an adventure darkens when it becomes evident that a volatile ex-con, Asa Watts (Bruce Dern), and his gang of cattle rustlers are following them.

Top: Wil Andersen (Wayne) and his new hands get acquainted. Bottom: Andersen delivers a history lesson to Cimarron (A. Martinez) as they pass through Little Big Horn.

Director Mark Rydell hired rodeo performers as well as actors to fill a young cast that was mostly as green as the characters. For Martinez, working with his father's favorite actor was surreal. The 20-year-old remembered nights spent in his pajamas at the drive-in watching Wayne's films, and now the legendary star was teaching him how to fight in the movies. "He's just like John Wayne on-screen. He doesn't do anything different, and when he finds out you're having trouble, he gets in there and helps you," said 13-year-old co-star Mike Pyeatt.

The kids were not the only ones dazzled by the western icon. Dern, an Actor's Studio alumni, was delighted to discover that while Wayne might not be a Method actor, he was a kindred spirit. "He made you go out on the edge, dare, risk," Dern recalled. "The one thing I remember about him more than anything else is he insisted that you push the envelope."

Critics disapproved of *The Cowboys'* tonal shift from coming-of-age yarn to violent shoot'em up. Roger Ebert's review in the *Chicago Sun-Times* was typical as he praised Wayne's "solid" performance, but lamented, "It's a shame they had to go for the unlikely, violent, and totally contrived last 30 minutes." The film went on to gross only $7.5 million at the box office; 30 years later, however, Dern put *The Cowboys* into perspective: "I felt that I was part of the last great western."

Top: Andersen and Asa Watts (Bruce Dern) face off as the cowboys watch. Bottom: Andersen's cowboys.

THE TRAIN ROBBERS (1973)

WARNER BROS. PICTURES

DIRECTOR: BURT KENNEDY

SCREENPLAY: KENNEDY

PRINCIPAL CAST: JOHN WAYNE (LANE), ANN-MARGRET (MRS. LOWE), ROD TAYLOR (GRADY), BEN JOHNSON (JESSE), CHRISTOPHER GEORGE (CALHOUN), BOBBY VINTON (BEN), JERRY GATLIN (SAM) AND RICARDO MONTALBAN (PINKERTON MAN)

The Train Robbers is a genial, unhurried, folksy western, conceived and designed to harken to an era of kinder, gentler filmmaking. John Wayne was dismayed by the cynical, blood-drenched westerns of Sam Peckinpah and Sergio Leone and disgusted by the takeover of Hollywood studios by enormous corporations with no affinity for the film business. Now in the twilight of his legendary career, Wayne saw himself as perhaps the last actor upholding a screen tradition of moral certitude and good old-fashioned American values. The rasp in his voice and the stiffness in his movements (thanks to the two ribs he fractured before production commenced) only enhanced the feeling that the golden age of the western had passed.

The plot is as straightforward and uncomplicated as it gets: Lane (Wayne) has enlisted a pair of old pals (Rod Taylor and Ben Johnson) from his Civil War days and some young guns (Christopher George, Bobby

Top: The gang — Ben (Bobby Vinton), Sam (Jerry Gatlin), Calhoun (Christopher George), Grady (Rod Taylor) and Jesse (Ben Johnson) — meets Lane's train. Bottom: Mrs. Lowe (Ann-Margret) throws down the gauntlet to Lane (John Wayne).

Vinton and Jerry Gatlin) to track down $500,000 in hidden gold on behalf of Mrs. Lowe (Ann-Margret), who claims to be the widow of the man who stole it from the railroad. "It's something to do," Grady (Taylor) remarks good-humoredly, and that's a good deal of the motivation driving the characters and the film. It's only a slight exaggeration to say that nobody's here to make their fortune or their career — they're really along for a ride with the Duke. As a result, *The Train Robbers* is distinguished by the principals' easygoing camaraderie and abundance of laconic charm.

In *The Train Robbers*, Lane always behaves like a gentleman toward Mrs. Lowe, while on the set the star was typically generous to his female co-star. For her part, Ann-Margret pulls off the neat trick of being convincing as a woman of the 1880s while exhibiting an independent flair in tune with women of the 1970s. Mrs. Lowe is even prickly on occasion, at least in the context of a film that prominently features a shot of a rainbow. That's hardly an image one associates with a John Wayne picture, but as the *New York Times* critic Roger Greenspun wrote, "As an exercise in pleasantness, *The Train Robbers* is an interesting addition to the late history of the traditional unpretentious western."

Top: Calhoun and Lane set eyes on the coveted gold chest. Bottom: Mrs. Lowe and Lane catch their breath between gunfights.

McQ (1974)

WARNER BROS. PICTURES

DIRECTOR: JOHN STURGES

SCREENPLAY: LAWRENCE ROMAN

PRINCIPAL CAST: JOHN WAYNE (DETECTIVE LIEUTENANT LON McQ),
EDDIE ALBERT (CAPTAIN ED KOSTERMAN), DIANA MULDAUR (LOIS
BOYLE), COLLEEN DEWHURST (MYRA), CLU GULAGER (FRANKLIN
TOMS), DAVID HUDDLESTON (EDWARD "PINKY" FARROW), AL
LETTIERI (MANNY SANTIAGO) AND JULIE ADAMS (ELAINE FORRESTER)

John Wayne played plenty of Old West lawmen, but never a contemporary cop until *McQ*. Meant to capitalize on the success of films like *Dirty Harry* (1971), the crime drama failed to set the box office on fire. Audiences expected a hero with Clint Eastwood's tough sleekness. The elderly Wayne, 67 and struggling with his weight, did not meet the criteria. *McQ* is a movie that has improved with age, as Wayne's understated performance quietly dominates the screen.

When his partner Stan Boyle (William Bryant) is shot dead, Seattle police detective Lon McQ (John Wayne) suspects that local drug kingpin Manny Santiago (Al Lettieri) ordered the killing but his boss, Captain Ed Kosterman (Eddie Albert), pins the murder on hippie radicals. Obsessed with solving the deadly mystery, McQ leaves the force to pursue his leads as a private investigator.

Lon McQ's resemblance to Dirty Harry Callahan was no accident. Dirty Harry was a part that the Duke let slip through his fingers. When the *Dirty Harry* script came his way, Wayne was busy with other movies and he

Top: Detective Lon McQ (Wayne) comforts Lois (Diana Muldaur), the widow of his slain partner. Bottom: McQ pays a visit to his ex-wife, Elaine (Julie Adams).

did not want to accept a role that had been offered to Frank Sinatra first. But he also confessed to misreading the character. "I thought Harry was a rogue cop," he revealed. "Put that down to narrow-mindedness, because when I saw the picture I realized Harry was the kind of part I'd played often enough; a guy who lives within the law, but breaks the rules when he really has to in order to save others."

McQ was Wayne's chance to prove he could play a hardboiled, modern man. *Dirty Harry* brought the .357 Magnum into the public consciousness. *McQ* would do the same for the MAC-10 submachine gun. It did not quite work out that way. Set to Elmer Bernstein's jazzy score and full of muscular action scenes, the attempt to follow *Dirty Harry*'s path met with mostly derision. "Prostratingly dull," sniffed the *New Yorker*'s Pauline Kael. "The action sequences are frequent but arthritic," wrote *Time*. "Wildly undramatic," the *New York Times'* Nora Sayre pronounced.

Variety offered the rare rave, "A good contemporary crime actioner…*McQ* attracts and sustains continued interest from the opening frames." Audiences were unconvinced, as *McQ* earned only $4.1 million at the box office. "The cop no one can stop. Even the cops," read *McQ*'s tagline, but its star proved to be less invincible. Wayne would play a modern cop again in *Brannigan* (1975), but he would retreat to *Rooster Cogburn* (1975) and *The Shootist* (1976), ending his career as he'd begun it — back in the saddle.

Top: John Wayne plays a police detective for the first time in his long career in *McQ*. Bottom: McQ's unorthodox ways meet with resistance from Captain Kosterman (Eddie Albert) while Councilman Toms (Clu Gulager) tries to run interference.

BRANNIGAN (1975)

UNITED ARTISTS

DIRECTOR: DOUGLAS HICKOX

SCREENPLAY: CHRISTOPHER TRUMBO, MICHAEL BUTLER, WILLIAM P. MCGIVERN AND WILLIAM W. NORTON

PRINCIPAL CAST: JOHN WAYNE (LIEUTENANT JIM BRANNIGAN), RICHARD ATTENBOROUGH (COMMANDER SWANN), JUDY GEESON (SERGEANT JENNIFER THATCHER), MEL FERRER (MEL FIELDS) AND JOHN VERNON (BEN LARKIN)

As the western genre faded in popularity, John Wayne followed the lead of Clint Eastwood and attempted to reinvent himself as the star of two urban crime dramas, *McQ* (1974) and *Brannigan*. In the latter, he plays the title role, a rough-and-tumble Chicago cop who brings his own brand of rough justice to staid Great Britain.

A team of four writers concocted this derivative "fish-out-of-water" police yarn, which takes Lieutenant Jim Brannigan (Wayne) from the Windy City to London, where he is to collect fugitive mobster Ben Larkin (John Vernon). Before Brannigan and his Scotland Yard minders Swann (Richard Attenborough) and DS Jennifer Thatcher (Jennifer Geeson) can arrest Larkin, however, he's kidnapped. Further complications arise when it becomes evident that a hit man has trailed Brannigan to England.

That summer of 1974 was a difficult time for Wayne. His two-decade-long marriage to third wife Pilar was

Top: Angell (Arthur Batanides) gets the drop on Chicago cop Jim Brannigan (Wayne). Bottom: DS Jennifer Thatcher (Judy Geeson) shows Brannigan a little tenderness.

disintegrating and his health was beginning to fade. As to *Brannigan*, he had no illusions about the caliber of the film. "It's the same old western brought up to date," he said.

Although he wasn't thrilled by the material, Wayne thoroughly enjoyed working with Geeson and Attenborough. As he told journalist Michael Munn, "Judy's young enough to be my daughter. A lovely girl. I like the irony of the script that she's trying to look after me." Attenborough similarly amused him, as Wayne shared with Munn: "He's a funny guy. He comes across all upper-crust, but he's got a wonderful sense of humor."

Unfortunately Wayne's attempt to join Clint Eastwood as an urban action hero failed, due to the mediocre script and director Douglas Hickox's bland direction. In his book *John Wayne's America: The Politics of Celebrity*, historian Garry Wills dismisses *Brannigan* as "a kind of *Slightly Soiled Harry*." Reviews were generally poor, even as they praised Wayne's performance, with Roger Ebert in the *Chicago Sun-Times* writing, "[Wayne] acts it with such sincerity that we understand what a star is, even while we're forming doubts about the movie." *Time* derided the film's "incompetencies," but mused, "Maybe one of our Bicentennial projects ought to be a search for a movie worthy of a national treasure like John Wayne." Ironically, the star did find that dream project with his final film, *The Shootist* (1976) — a return to the western with *Dirty Harry*'s director Don Siegel.

Top: Brannigan's latest chase ends with a wrecked sports car and the opportunity for some sightseeing.
Bottom: Brannigan's quest for justice leads to a shootout.

ROOSTER COGBURN (1975)

UNIVERSAL PICTURES

DIRECTOR: STUART MILLAR

SCREENPLAY: MARTHA HYER (AS MARTIN JULIEN)

PRINCIPAL CAST: JOHN WAYNE (ROOSTER COGBURN), KATHARINE HEPBURN (EULA GOODNIGHT), ANTHONY ZERBE (BREED), JOHN McINTIRE (JUDGE PARKER), STROTHER MARTIN (SHANGHAI McCOY), RICHARD ROMANCITO (WOLF) AND RICHARD JORDAN (HAWK)

Six years after he played the one-eyed, whiskey-swilling federal marshal in *True Grit* (1969), Wayne donned the character's eye patch once again in *Rooster Cogburn*. This much-ballyhooed sequel to Henry Hathaway's classic western paired Wayne with fellow screen icon Katharine Hepburn, but for a film starring two bona-fide Hollywood legends, *Rooster Cogburn* falls short of expectations.

Borrowing freely from the plots of both *True Grit* and *The African Queen* (1951), *Rooster Cogburn* opens in 1880, as Cogburn loses his federal marshal badge due to his reckless ways. However, when the outlaw Hawk (Richard Jordan) steals a wagon full of nitroglycerin, the local judge reinstates Cogburn and sends him after the thief. On the trail, Cogburn comes across missionary Eula Goodnight (Hepburn) burying her father. When she learns that Rooster is hunting Hawk, the killer of her father, Eula insists that he take her and the Native American boy Wolf (Richard Romancito) with him.

Top: Rooster Cogburn (Wayne) pleads his own case to a courtroom judge. Bottom: As her father (Jon Lormer) watches in fear, Eula Goodnight (Hepburn) stands her ground as Hawk (Richard Jordan) shoots bullets near her feet.

At first, the hard-drinking Cogburn balks at the prospect of teetotaling Eula as a traveling companion, but she refuses to take no for answer. As they set forth in pursuit of Hawk, the unlikely duo gradually learn to appreciate each other and form a close friendship.

Written by actress Martha Hyer under the pen name of Martin Julien, *Rooster Cogburn* pales in comparison to *True Grit*; there's a workmanlike quality to the screenplay and Stuart Millar's direction that undermines what could have been a grandly entertaining old-fashioned western. Happily, Wayne and Hepburn are so winning together that the film's flaws ultimately don't matter. As Vincent Canby of the *New York Times* wrote, "It's a cheerful, throwaway western, featuring two stars of the grand tradition who respond to each other with verve that makes the years disappear."

On location in Oregon, Hepburn threw herself into the role of Eula, even doing most of her stunt work. As the 68-year-old actress explained, "I haven't waited all these years to a do a cowboy picture with John Wayne to give up a single minute of it now." In contrast, Wayne struggled with declining health during the filming of *Rooster Cogburn*, but Hepburn's enthusiasm left him besotted: "How she must have been at age 25 or 30! How lucky a man would have been to have found her then!"

Top: Eula explains that she must come along, much to Rooster's chagrin. Bottom: Rooster and Eula get their first look at the rapids straight ahead.

THE SHOOTIST (1976)

PARAMOUNT PICTURES

DIRECTOR: DON SIEGEL

SCREENPLAY: MILES HOOD SWARTHOUT AND SCOTT HALE

BASED ON THE NOVEL BY GLENDON SWARTHOUT

PRINCIPAL CAST: JOHN WAYNE (J.B. BOOKS), LAUREN BACALL (BOND ROGERS), RON HOWARD (GILLOM ROGERS), JAMES STEWART (DR. E.W. HOSTETLER), RICHARD BOONE (MIKE SWEENEY), HUGH O'BRIEN (JACK PULFORD), HARRY MORGAN (MARSHAL J. WALTER THIBIDO), SHEREE NORTH (SEREPTA), RICK LENZ (DAN DOBKINS) AND JOHN CARRADINE (HEZEKIAH BECKHUM)

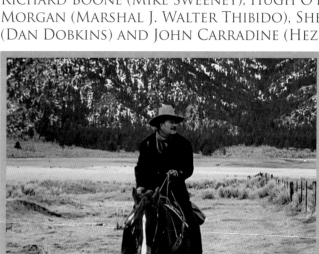

John Wayne saved the best for last. *The Shootist* may not rank as his finest film, but he never had a better role than that of titular gunslinger J.B. Books. "When the legend becomes fact, print the legend," was the credo from one of Wayne's great westerns, *The Man Who Shot Liberty Valance* (1962). In *The Shootist*, an adaptation of Glendon Swarthout's novel, legend and fact merge as character and star share both a dire prognosis and one final shot at leaving the stage on their own terms. It is an extraordinarily moving coda to Wayne's lengthy career.

Siegel perfectly encapsulates the gunslinger's life and his star's career in the first moments of *The Shootist*, as footage of a young, sepia-toned Wayne and scenes from *Hondo* (1953), *Rio Bravo* (1959), and *El Dorado* (1966) unreel, leading up to the introduction of the elderly Books. The 1901 model is weathered and broader than the lean youth of 1871, but he looks hale and hearty. That rosy health is an illusion, as Carson City doctor E.W. Hostetler (James Stewart) confirms that Books is dying of cancer.

Top: Shootist J.B. Books (Wayne) making his last ride out of the mountains. Bottom: Books and Doc Hostetler (James Stewart) talk over a terrible diagnosis.

However dire the prognosis, Books is used to managing his own destiny. Securing a room in a boarding house run by the widowed Bond Rogers (Lauren Bacall), he sets about setting his affairs in order, no easy feat in a town in which his reputation as a killer makes him both a target and a celebrity. Old enemies have scores to settle. Rival shootists know that taking him down would gild their reputations. Newspaperman Dan Dobkins (Rick Lenz) wants to make a name for himself by writing up Books's exploits. Serepta (Sheree North), an old girlfriend, is looking for security. Only the initially cool Mrs. Rogers and her worshipful teenage son Gillom (Ron Howard) treat the man with genuine human feeling.

The Duke's battle with cancer during the 1960s was the stuff of legend. He had lost a lung, but just as his western heroes defeated the villains, so had Wayne conquered the disease. But by the mid-1970s, the word in Hollywood was that his health was precarious again. A measure of what he meant to his peers can be taken by how quickly *The Shootist*'s supporting cast filled out. Producers William Self and Mike Frankovich were not even considering an all-star cast on their modest $8 million budget, but cognizant that this could well be Wayne's swan song, luminaries like Richard Boone, John Carradine and the actor's close friend Stewart lined up to take part.

Hugh O'Brien, who played a fellow shootist in the film, was among those eager to act alongside Wayne. "I

Top: Books and Mrs. Rogers (Lauren Bacall) share a moment of domesticity. Bottom: "Make like it's a nipple." Books makes known his displeasure of nosy newspaperman Dan Dobkins (Rick Lenz).

said, 'You don't have to pay me. I just want to be in the film," he remembered.

Ironically, it was Wayne who very nearly did not get the role of a lifetime. While Siegel insisted, "No one in the world could play the leading role of J.B. Books but John Wayne," producer Self admitted that he and Frankovich initially offered the part to George C. Scott. They knew that Wayne was ill and they were not sure that he even wanted to work, but the actor read the script and knew it was for him. "I think he understood this character and maybe that was due to his own problems with cancer," Self theorized.

As the producers feared, Wayne's health faltered during the production. His physical condition even dictated where Siegel could shoot his opening scene of Books riding out of the mountains. He found the perfect location near Carson City, but at 6,000 feet, the air was too thin for Wayne's decreased lung capacity. Siegel's team eventually found a spot at 3,500 feet, but even that was too high as far as the actor's doctors were concerned. Siegel lied, saying the location was at 3,000 feet in order to get the shot he wanted. That was trivial compared to what was coming when Wayne, a consummate professional, was simply too ill to work for several days. Siegel was able to shoot around him, but the situation was so

"I won't be wronged, I won't be insulted, and I won't be laid a hand to. I don't do those things to other people and I require the same of them."

— J.B. Books' (Wayne)

Books and Mrs. Rogers go for a ride and contemplate what might have been.

Gillom Rogers (Ron Howard) gets a shooting lesson from a consummate pro.

critical that Frankovich asked the director if he could complete the film if the star could not continue.

Eventually, Wayne recovered enough to finish the picture, returning ornery enough to demand that Siegel reshoot a scene in which Books shoots another character in the back. O'Brien watched the rushes with the actor and 25 years later vividly recalled Wayne's horrified reaction: "Wait a damn minute! I've done 265 films. I've never shot anybody in the back and I don't intend to start now. You reshoot it — otherwise, you get yourself another boy."

The year 1976 produced *Rocky, Network,* and *All the President's Men.* Perhaps *The Shootist* was simply too out of step with the 1970s-era sensibility. Reviews were mixed. Richard Eder in the *New York Times* sneeringly dismissed it as "third in a wave of geriatric westerns that have afforded new employment for the wrinkles and creases of John Wayne." *Time*'s Jay Cocks carped, "It is hampered by a sentimental, overwrought script and, finally, by its own reserve." But Roger Ebert wrote in the *Chicago Sun-Times,* "Unless you have already discovered that John Wayne is an actor as well as a movie star, you will be surprised by the dimensions he provides for

"It isn't always about being fast or even accurate that counts. It's being willing. I found out early that most men regardless of cause or need aren't willing. They blink an eye or draw a breath before they'll pull a trigger. I won't."

— J.B. Books (Wayne)

J.B. Books." *Variety* raved, "*The Shootist* stands as one of John Wayne's towering achievements. Don Siegel's terrific film is simply beautiful." Audiences were similarly of two minds. On the one hand, Wayne won the People's Choice Award four times running, from the award's inception in 1975 through 1979, but *The Shootist* earned just over $8 million at the box office, barely earning back its production costs.

Wayne passed away three years later on June 11, 1979, finally losing his long battle with cancer. When he died, Roger Ebert wrote in his obituary, "If they play a movie on the *Late Show* in tribute to John Wayne, *The Shootist* would make a good one." Decades later, that sentiment still rings true, as the movie stands a fitting farewell to a star and his vibrant career.

Books enjoys a birthday drink before the shooting starts.

"I'm a dying man who's afraid of the dark."

— J.B. Books (Wayne)

174

"John Wayne was J.B. Books. They both suffered from an incurable cancer. They were as one in bravery, temper, sense of humor, short-temperedness, and kindness to those who proved worthy of their kindness."

— Director Don Siegel

Top: Gillom puts his shooting lesson to use when he comes to Books' aid. Bottom: Books' face reflects the pain of disease and bullets.

FILMOGRAPHY

Brown of Harvard (1926)
Bardelys the Magnificent (1926)
The Great K&A Robbery (1926)
Annie Laurie (1927)
The Drop Kick (1927)
Mother Machree (1928)
Hangman's House (1928)
Salute (1929)
Words and Music (1929)
Men Without Women (1930)
Rough Romance (1930)
Cheer Up and Smile (1930)
The Big Trail (1930)
Girls Demand Excitement (1931)
Three Girls Lost (1931)
Men Are Like That (1931)
Range Feud (1931)
Maker of Men (1931)
Haunted Gold (1932)
Shadow of the Eagle (1932)
Hurricane Express (1932)
Texas Cyclone (1932)
Lady and Gent (1932)
Two-Fisted Law (1932)
Ride Him, Cowboy (1932)
The Big Stampede (1932)
The Telegraph Trail (1933)
Central Airport (1933)
His Private Secretary (1933)
Somewhere in Sonora (1933)
Life of Jimmy Dolan (1933)
The Three Musketeers (1933)
Baby Face (1933)
The Man from Monterey (1933)
Riders of Destiny (1933)
Sagebrush Trail (1933)
West of the Divide (1933)
Lucky Texan (1934)
Blue Steel (1934)
The Man from Utah (1934)
Randy Rides Alone (1934)
The Star Packer (1934)
The Trail Beyond (1934)
'Neath Arizona Skies (1934)
Lawless Frontier (1935)
Texas Terror (1935)
Rainbow Valley (1935)
Paradise Canyon (1935)
The Dawn Rider (1935)
Westward Ho (1935)
Desert Trail (1935)
New Frontier (1935)
Lawless Range (1935)

The Lawless Nineties (1936)
King of the Pecos (1936)
The Oregon Trail (1936)
Winds of the Wasteland (1936)
The Sea Spoilers (1936)
The Lonely Trail (1936)
Conflict (1936)
California Straight Ahead (1937)
I Cover the War (1937)
Idol of the Crowds (1937)
Adventure's End (1937)
Born to the West (1938)
Pals of the Saddle (1938)
Overland Stage Raiders (1938)
Santa Fe Stampede (1938)
Red River Range (1938)
Stagecoach (1939)
The Night Riders (1939)
Three Texas Steers (1939)
Wyoming Outlaw (1939)
New Frontier (1939)
Allegheny Uprising (1939)
Dark Command (1940)
Three Faces West (1940)
The Long Voyage Home (1940)
Seven Sinners (1940)
A Man Betrayed (1941)
Lady from Louisiana (1941)
The Shepherd of the Hills (1941)
Lady for a Night (1941)
Reap the Wild Wind (1942)
The Spoilers (1942)
In Old California (1942)
Flying Tigers (1942)
Reunion in France (1942)
Pittsburgh (1942)
Lady Takes a Chance (1943)
War of the Wildcats (1943)
The Fighting Seabees (1944)
Tall in the Saddle (1944)
Flame of the Barbary Coast (1945)
Back to Bataan (1945)
Dakota (1945)
They Were Expendable (1945)
Without Reservations (1946)
Angel and the Badman (1947)
Tycoon (1947)
Fort Apache (1948)
Red River (1948)
3 Godfathers (1948)
Wake of the Red Witch (1948)
She Wore a Yellow Ribbon (1949)
The Fighting Kentuckian (1949)

Sands of Iwo Jima (1949)
Rio Grande (1950)
Operation Pacific (1951)
Flying Leathernecks (1951)
The Quiet Man (1952)
Big Jim McLain (1952)
Trouble Along the Way (1953)
Island in the Sky (1953)
Hondo (1953)
The High and the Mighty (1954)
The Sea Chase (1955)
Blood Alley (1955)
The Conqueror (1956)
The Searchers (1956)
The Wings of Eagles (1957)
Jet Pilot (1957)
Legend of the Lost (1957)
I Married a Woman (1958)
The Barbarian and the Geisha (1958)
Rio Bravo (1959)
The Horse Soldiers (1959)
The Alamo (1960)
North to Alaska (1960)
The Comancheros (1961)
The Man Who Shot Liberty Valance (1962)
Hatari (1962)
The Longest Day (1962)
How the West Was Won (1962)
Donovan's Reef (1963)
McLintock! (1963)
Circus World (1964)
The Greatest Story Ever Told (1965)
In Harm's Way (1965)
The Sons of Katie Elder (1965)
Cast a Giant Shadow (1966)
War Wagon (1967)
El Dorado (1967)
The Green Berets (1968)
Hellfighters (1968)
True Grit (1969)
The Undefeated (1969)
Chisum (1970)
Rio Lobo (1970)
Big Jake (1971)
The Cowboys (1972)
The Train Robbers (1973)
Cahill, United States Marshal (1973)
McQ (1974)
Brannigan (1975)
Rooster Cogburn (1975)
The Shootist (1976)